access

D0279246

EUROPE *and the* COLD WAR, 1945–91

a c c e s s   t o   h i s t o r y

EUROPE *and the* COLD WAR, 1945–91

David Williamson

Hodder & Stoughton

A MEMBER OF THE HODDER HEADLINE GROUP

Acknowledgements

The cover illustration shows a nucleur explosion over Bikini atoll, reproduced courtesy of Corbis.

The publishers would like to thank the following individuals, institutions and companies for permission to reproduce copyright illustrations in this book: © Bettmann/Corbis, pages 62, 83 and 101; © Hulton Getty, page 97; Christmas card by Kem, courtesy of Alexander and Richard Marengo/Centre for the Study of Cartoons and Caricature, University of Kent, Canterbury, page 35; © Owen Franken/Corbis, page 119; © Presse und Informationsamt der Bundesregierung, pages 85 and 126; Royal Air Force Museum, Hendon, page 63.

The publishers would also like to thank the following for permission to reproduce copyright material in this volume:

The Brookings Institution for the extract from *The Great Transition: American–Soviet Relations and the End of the Cold War* by R.L. Garthoff, 1994; CWIHP (Cold War International History Project) for the extracts from *The Warsaw Pact and the Polish Crisis of 1980–81* by M. Kramer, *Working Notes from the session of the CPSU CC Presidium on 31.10.1956, Point VI of Protocol No. 49* in *CWIHP Bulletin, When Did the Cold War End?* by T. Blanton, *Ullricht and the Concrete Rose: New Archival Evidence on the Dynamics of Soviet–East German Relations and the Berlin Crisis, 1958–61* by H. Harrison; Duncker and Humblot for the extract from volume 12 of *In Studien zur Deutschlandfrage* by S. Suckut, Duncker and Humblot, 1993; HarperCollins Publishers for the extract from *Democracy in America* by Alexis De Tocqueville, ed. J.P. Mayer and Max Lerner, trans. George Lawrence, English translation copyright © 1965 by Harper & Row, Publishers, Inc.; Macmillan Ltd for the extracts from 'The Soviet Union and the Berlin Crisis' by M.M. Narinskii in *The Soviet Union and Europe* edited by F. Gori and S. Pons, Macmillan, 1996, and *Stalin's Unwanted Child: The Soviet Union, the German Question and the Founding of the GDR* by W. Loth, Macmillan, 1998; Martin Gilbert for the extract from *Second World War* by Martin Gilbert, Phoenix, 2001; the extract from *Present at the Creation: My Years in the State Department* by Dean Acheson. Copyright © 1969 by Dean Acheson. Used by permission of W.W. Norton & Co. Inc.; Pearson Education for the extract from *The Origins of the Cold War* by M. McCauley, Longman, 1983; Routledge for the extract from *The Soviet Union in World Politics* by G. Roberts, Routledge, 1999; the extract from *The Berlin Crisis, 1958–1962* by J. Schick. Copyright © 1971 Trustees of the University of Pennsylvania. Reprinted with permission of the University of Pennsylvania Press.

Every effort has been made to trace and acknowledge ownership of copyright. The publishers will be glad to make suitable arrangements with any copyright holders whom it has not been possible to contact.

Orders: please contact Bookpoint Ltd, 130 Milton Park, Abingdon, Oxon OX14 4SB. Telephone (44) 01235 827720, Fax: (44) 01235 400454. Lines are open from 9.00–6.00, Monday to Saturday, with a 24 hour message answering service. Email address: orders@bookpoint.co.uk

British Library Cataloguing in Publication Data
A catalogue record for this title is available from the British Library

ISBN 0 340 772743

First published 2001
Impression number   10 9 8 7 6 5 4 3 2 1
Year   2007 2006 2005 2004 2003 2002 2001

Copyright © 2001 David Williamson

Typeset by Fakenham Photosetting Limited, Fakenham, Norfolk
Printed in Great Britain for Hodder & Stoughton Educational, a division of Hodder Headline Plc, 338 Euston Road, London NW1 3BH by Bath Press, England.

Contents

Preface

To the general reader

Although the *Access to History* series has been designed with the needs of students studying the subject at higher examination levels very much in mind, it also has a great deal to offer the general reader. The main body of the text (i.e. ignoring the 'Study Guides' at the ends of chapters) forms a readable and yet stimulating survey of a coherent topic as studied by historians. However, each author's aim has not merely been to provide a clear explanation of what happened in the past (to interest and inform): it has also been assumed that most readers wish to be stimulated into thinking further about the topic and to form opinions of their own about the significance of the events that are described and discussed (to be challenged). Thus, although no prior knowledge of the topic is expected on the reader's part, she or he is treated as an intelligent and thinking person throughout. The author tends to share ideas and possibilities with the reader, rather than passing on numbers of so-called 'historical truths'.

To the student reader

This title ensures the results of recent research are reflected in the text and includes features aimed at assisting you in your study of the topic at AS Level, A Level and Higher. Two features are designed to assist you during your first reading of a chapter. The *Points to Consider* section following each chapter title is intended to focus your attention on the main theme(s) of the chapter, and the issues box following most section headings alerts you to the question or questions to be dealt with in the section. The *Working on...* section at the end of each chapter suggests ways of gaining maximum benefit from the chapter.

There are many ways in which the series can be used by students studying History at a higher level. It will, therefore, be worthwhile thinking about your own study strategy before you start your work on this book. Obviously, your strategy will vary depending on the aim you have in mind, and the time for study that is available to you.

If, for example, you want to acquire a general overview of the topic in the shortest possible time, the following approach will probably be the most effective:

1. Read Chapter 1. As you do so, keep in mind the issues raised in the *Points to Consider* section.
2. Read the *Points to Consider* section at the beginning of Chapter 2 and decide whether it is necessary for you to read this chapter.
3. If it is, read the chapter, stopping at each heading or sub-heading to note down the main points that have been made. Often, the best way of doing this is to answer the question(s) posed in the Key Issues boxes.

4. Repeat stage 2 (and stage 3 where appropriate) for all the other chapters.

If, however, your aim is to gain a thorough grasp of the topic, taking however much time is necessary to do so, you may benefit from carrying out the same procedure with each chapter, as follows:

1. Try to read the chapter in one sitting. As you do this, bear in mind any advice given in the *Points to Consider* section.
2. Study the flow diagram at the end of the chapter, ensuring that you understand the general 'shape' of what you have just read.
3. Read the *Working on...* section and decide what further work you need to do on the chapter. In particularly important sections of the book, this is likely to involve reading the chapter a second time and stopping at each heading and sub-heading to think about (and probably to write a summary of) what you have just read.
4. Attempt the *Source-based questions* section. It will sometimes be sufficient to think through your answers, but additional understanding will often be gained by forcing yourself to write them down.

When you have finished the main chapters of the book, study the 'Further Reading' section and decide what additional reading (if any) you will do on the topic.

This book has been designed to help make your studies both enjoyable and successful. If you can think of ways in which this could have been done more effectively, please contact us. In the meantime, we hope that you will gain greatly from your study of History.

Keith Randell & Robert Pearce

1 The Cold War: An Introduction

POINTS TO CONSIDER

The point of this introductory chapter is to help you understand the overall pattern of events before studying the various phases of the Cold War in Europe in greater detail. Consequently it introduces you to the main events and themes of the Cold War. It gives you an idea as to when it started, in what ways it developed and changed between 1945 and 1989 and how historians have interpreted it.

KEY DATES

1917	Russian Revolution.
1918	Wilson's 14 Points.
1945	End of Second World War.
1947	Truman Doctrine and Marshall Plan.
1948–9	Berlin Blockade.
1953	Death of Stalin.
1958–61	Second Berlin Crisis.
1968	Invasion of Czechoslovakia by Warsaw Pact Forces.
1970	SALT talks begin.
1971	Four Power Agreement on Berlin.
1975	Helsinki Final Act.
1979	USSR invades Afghanistan.
1983	Pershing and Cruise missiles installed in Western Europe.
1989	Berlin Wall breached.
1990	Germany re-united.

1 What Was the Cold War?

> **KEY ISSUES** What are the main characteristics of the Cold War and how many Cold Wars were there?

The term 'cold war' had been used before 1945 to describe periods of extreme tension between states stopping just short of war. In 1893 the German socialist, Eduard Bernstein, described the arms race between Germany and its neighbours as a kind of 'cold war' where 'there is no shooting but ... bleeding'.[1] In 1945 when the USA and the USSR faced each other eyeball to eyeball in Germany this term rapidly came back into fashion. The British writer, George Orwell, commenting on the significance of the dropping of the atom bomb foresaw 'a peace that is no peace', in which the USA and USSR would be both 'unconquerable and in a permanent state of cold war' with each other.[2] The Cold War was, however, more than just an arms race. It was also, as the historian John Mason has pointed out, 'a fundamental clash of ideologies and interests'.[3] Essentially the USSR followed Lenin's and Marx's teaching that conflict between Communism and Capitalism was unavoidable, while the USA and its allies for much of the time saw the USSR, in the words of President Reagan in 1983, as an 'evil empire', intent on the destruction of democracy and civil rights.

Central Europe in 1955

CAPITALISM AND COMMUNISM

In its purest form Capitalism is an economic system in which the production of goods and their distribution depend on the investment of private capital (money) with a view to making a profit. A capitalist economy is run by individuals, who wish to make a profit from their businesses or capital, rather than by the state. By the 1940s in the Western World the period of 'pure capitalism' was over and the state was playing an increasingly major role in directing key sections of the economy, although not on the same scale as in the USSR.

Communism is profoundly hostile to capitalism. It sees it as an evil scheme for exploiting the working classes and believes that liberal parliamentary democracy with its political parties and regular elections is a sham which conceals the controlling role of big business and capital in society. It therefore puts forward the idea of a class war waged against the owners of capital, which will lead initially to all property, businesses and industry being owned by the state. At first there will be a dictatorship of the workers and then this will melt away and a true Communist society will emerge in which 'each gives according to their ability to those according to their need'. An attractive theory, but, as seemed only too clear to the West, hardly carried out by Stalin in the USSR!

The American historian, Anders Stephanson[4] has defined the essence of the Cold War as follows:

- Both sides denied each other's legitimacy as a regime and attempted to attack each other by every means short of war.
- Increasingly this conflict became bipolar, that is say a struggle between the two great Superpowers, the USA and USSR.
- There was an intense build up of both nuclear and conventional military weapons and a prolonged arms race.
- Each side suppressed its internal dissidents.

Most historians would more or less accept this definition, although there is less agreement on the time-scale of the Cold War. David Reynolds, whose chronology is for the most part followed in this book, argues that there were three cold wars, 1948–53, 1958–63 and 1979–85, 'punctured by periods of *détente*',[5] or easing of tension. Two Russian historians, Vladislav Zubok and Constantine Pleshakov, however, provide a slightly different model: they define the Cold War as lasting from 1948 to the Cuban Crisis of 1962 and the subsequent 27 years as a 'prolonged armistice'.[6] While the chronology of the Cold War is open to debate, and the beginning of the 'Second Cold War' could as easily be dated from October 1956 as from November 1958, it is important to grasp that the years 1945–89 formed a 'Cold War era', in which years of intense hostility alternated with periods of *détente*, but, even then, the arms race and ideological competition between the two sides continued.

2 The Origins of the Cold War, 1917–45

> **KEY ISSUE** Does it make sense to talk about a Cold War in the interwar period?

The simultaneous expansion of Russia and America until they dominated the world had been foreseen as early as 1835 by the French historian, Alexis de Tocqueville, who pointed out that

1   There are now two great nations in the world, which, starting from different points, seem to be advancing toward the same goal: the Russians and the Anglo-Americans.... [E]ach seems called by some secret design of Providence one day to hold in its hands the destinies of half the
5   world.

It was the First World war that brought these two great states more closely into contact with each other. When the USA entered the war against Germany, they were briefly allies, but this changed dramatically once the Bolsheviks seized power in October 1917 and made peace with Germany. One historian, Howard Roffmann, argued that the Cold War 'proceeded from the very moment the Bolsheviks triumphed in Russia in 1917'.[7] There was certainly immediate hostility between Soviet Russia and the Western states, which initially tried to strangle Bolshevism at birth by intervening in the Russian civil war and backing the Whites. Ideologically, too, there was a clash between the ideas of President Wilson and Lenin. Wilson in his Fourteen Points of April 1918 presented an ambitious global programme for self-determination, free trade and collective security through a League of Nations, while Lenin preached world revolution and Communism. This clash marked the *ideological origins* of the Cold War, but if the meaning of a Cold War is interpreted along the lines of Stephanson's definition above, then there was no Cold War proper during the Twenties and Thirties. In 1920 America withdrew back into isolation and in the 1930s the USSR under Stalin increasingly concentrated on building up its military and industrial strength. This did not stop Moscow from attempting to undermine Capitalism and the British and French colonial empires through the Comintern, the international Communist organisation set up in 1919. In the late Twenties relations between Britain and the USSR were so bad that they have been described as the first Anglo-Soviet Cold War. Yet there was no 'bi-polar' line up. In the 1930s for most of the time the USSR and the

USA were on the sidelines, while the growing divide was between the Axis powers, Germany and Italy, and the Western democracies, Britain and France. Shortly before war broke out in 1939 the USSR secured its neutrality on highly favourable conditions through the Nazi-Soviet Pact. Thus by the end of 1939 de Tocqueville's prophecy still seemed to be, as John Gaddis has put it, 'a wild improbability'.[8]

It was Hitler who created the context for the Cold War, when he invaded Russia in June 1941 and then, just after the Japanese attack on Pearl Harbor, declared war on the USA. The subsequent defeat and occupation of Germany by the USSR and the Western Allies in 1945 at last brought the two Superpowers, the USSR and America, face to face. A few days before he committed suicide Hitler predicted that:

1 With the defeat of the Reich [Germany] and pending the emergence of the Asiatic, the African, and perhaps the South American nationalisms, there will remain in the world only two Great Powers capable of confronting each other – the United States and Soviet Russia. The laws of
5 history and geography will compel these two Powers to a trial of strength either military or in the fields of economics and ideology.

3 The Beginnings of the Cold War in Europe, 1945–48

> **KEY ISSUES** When did the Cold War start and which of the two Superpowers was more responsible for starting it?

The years 1945–48 saw the beginning of the Cold War in Europe, but historians cannot agree on who started it or on whether it could have been avoided. Most, however, do not dispute that it was a consequence of Hitler's defeat. This created a vacuum not only in Germany but in most of Continental Europe, which was filled by the armies of the wartime allies. The Russians occupied the whole of Eastern Europe up to the river Elbe, while the Americans, British and French dominated Western Europe, Greece and the Mediterranean (see map page 2). Inevitably the interests of the Great Powers, particularly of the USA and USSR, collided with each other in this vacuum. Some historians see this as the key explanation of the Cold War. Louis Halle, for instance, has likened the Cold War to placing a 'scorpion and a tarantula together in a bottle'.[9] This 'realist' interpretation does, of course, ignore the question of intention. 'Traditionalist' Western historians, such as Herbert Feiss, writing in the 1950s, firmly put the blame for starting the Cold War on Stalin. They argued that Stalin ignored promises given at the Yalta Conference in February 1945, to support democratically elected governments. Instead, he proceeded over the next three years to put his own Communist stooges in power in the Eastern European states. Once it was clear that Britain and France were too weak to defend Western Europe, the Americans then intervened and made the following key decisions, which in effect marked the beginning of the Cold War:

I. The Truman Doctrine of Spring 1947 offered military help to Greece and Turkey in their fight against Communism;

II. The Marshall Plan, announced in mid 1947, helped revive the Western economies and so block the spread of Communism;

III. In Germany the USA in the absence of any agreement with the USSR merged its zone of occupation with the British in January 1947, thereby creating Bizonia. In June 1948 the Western Allies introduced a new currency into their zones and made the crucial decision to set up a new West German state.

This interpretation of the start of the Cold War shows the USA responding *defensively* to aggressive Soviet moves. In the 1990s the historian, John Gaddis, has given a new slant to this interpretation by arguing that the Cold War was an unavoidable consequence of Stalin's paranoia (deep distrust), and was an extension of the way he dealt with opposition within the USSR.[10]

Revisionist historians writing in the 1960s and 1970s, however, argued that America and, to a lesser extent, Britain pursued policies, which in fact caused the Cold War in Europe. For instance, William Appleman Williams writing as early as 1959 claimed that Washington was aiming to force the USSR to join the global economy and open its frontiers to both American imports and political ideas, which would almost certainly have undermined the Stalinist regime.[11] Ten years later another historian, Gabriel Kolko, summed up American policy as aiming 'to restructure the world so that American business could trade, operate, and profit without restrictions everywhere'.[12]

Given the bipolar nature of the Cold War, historians initially concentrated on the USSR and America, yet in the early stages of the Cold War both Britain and France were still influential, although declining Powers. Recent research has shown how Britain played a major role in the division of Germany and in turning the offer of Marshall Aid into a practical economic recovery plan. The Cold War ultimately divided Europe into two great blocs, yet within Western Europe, as we shall see, the individual states were, to quote Reynolds, not just 'blank slates on which America could write a new history'.[13] Similarly in Eastern Europe historians are beginning to discover that local Communist politicians were at times also able to influence events, as was seen particularly in the events leading up to the building of the Berlin Wall (pages 103–04).

4 The 'First Cold War', 1948–53

> **KEY ISSUE** What events led to the formation of NATO and the Pleven Plan?

The years 1948–53 were a period of prolonged confrontation in Europe between the USA and USSR. From 1948, at the latest, it became clear that the Cold War in Europe essentially revolved around the German question. The Soviets were determined to stop the Americans and their Allies from building up a new and powerful state in West Germany. They therefore blockaded West Berlin, which was occupied by the three Western Allies, from June 1948 to May 1949 in the hope that they could force Washington to reverse this policy. They were thwarted because of the Anglo-American airlift, which managed to keep West Berlin supplied with food, clothing and raw materials right through the winter of 1948–9. The Berlin Crisis was the first major confrontation between the Americans and Russians. It reinforced the division of Germany and Europe and speeded up the arms race. In April 1949 the signing of the North Atlantic Treaty marked the foundation of a new Western alliance, while in July the Russians exploded their first atom bomb. The Federal Republic of Germany (FRG) was set up in September to be followed a month later by the Soviets establishing the German Democratic Republic (GDR).

The outbreak of the Korean war on 25 June 1950 led to demands for arming West Germany. Military needs and French fears of revived German power were reconciled through the Pleven Plan of October 1950, which proposed that West German soldiers should be integrated into a European Defence Community (army) (EDC). One of the consequences of the Cold War in Europe was that the former enemy states, Italy and (West) Germany, under American pressure, were gradually integrated both politically and economically into Western Europe, which was exactly what Stalin had hoped to avoid. In 1952 in an attempt to stop West German rearmament Stalin proposed setting up a free neutral Germany with its own army, but he failed to overcome the suspicions of either the Western Powers or the West Germans. During these years tension between the USSR and the Western Powers was dangerously high. Why then did war did not break out? Was it nuclear weapons that kept the peace or was Stalin in reality a cautious politician who was only too aware of the terrible losses the USSR had suffered in the Second World War?

5 The 'Thaw', 1953–57

> **KEY ISSUE** Can it be argued that 1953 was the end of the 'First Cold War'?

The death of Stalin marked a turning point in the Cold War in Europe. The Soviet leadership, absorbed in an internal power struggle, temporarily at least, wanted to relax tension with the Western Powers. It withdrew Soviet troops from Austria, but elsewhere the Iron Curtain (see page 45) remained firmly in place. When West Germany joined NATO in May 1955, the Russians responded by creating the Warsaw Pact, a military alliance composed of the USSR and the Eastern European satellite states.

The thaw confronted the Soviet leadership with a dilemma which it never solved. If it went too far down the line of destalinisation and liberalisation, it risked losing control of its satellites. Khrushchev's appeal for different 'national roads to Socialism' in 1956 fuelled demands for greater independence in both Poland and Hungary. In Poland these demands were partly satisfied, but in Hungary threats to withdraw from the Warsaw Pact and to end the domination of the Communist Party led to Soviet military intervention. The defeat of the Hungarian revolt showed both the limits to destalinisation and that the Western Allies would not intervene in what was regarded as a Soviet sphere of interest.

6 The 'Second Cold War', 1958–62

> **KEY ISSUE** Why can this period be called the 'Second Cold War'?

Although Europe's division was a reality by 1958, the balance of power in Germany was still precarious. The government of the GDR was hated by its population and only kept in place by Soviet bayonets. The FRG, on the other hand, was rapidly becoming a major European Power, and its growing prosperity exercised a magnet-like pull on the population of the GDR. Berlin was still under four Power control. As it was possible to cross unhindered from the Soviet to the Western Sectors of the city, between 1949 and 1958 well over 2.1 million East Germans out of a population of 17 million had escaped this way to the West. Inevitably this was a serious threat to the economic and social stability of the GDR.

The key to the dramatic increase in tension between 1958 and 1962 was Khrushchev's determination to use the impressive advances the USSR had made in missile technology to frighten the Western Powers into making concessions in Germany. The Berlin crisis began in November 1958, when Khrushchev demanded that West Berlin should become a 'free city' and that all Western troops should withdraw from it. He threatened further that if there was no agreement within six months, the USSR would sign a peace treaty with the GDR, which would enable it to control the access routes to West Berlin. Khrushchev in fact failed to carry out this threat, but he did allow the GDR to seal off East Berlin from the Western sectors on 13 August 1961 by the construction of what became known as the Berlin Wall. This effectively ended the crisis, although global tension reached a new peak in October 1962 when Khrushchev deployed nuclear missiles in Cuba to stop American attempts to overthrow the Communist regime of Fidel Castro. Only when he agreed to withdraw these after the most dangerous confrontation between the USA and USSR in the whole of the Cold War, was a way open for *détente* between the Superpowers in Europe.

7 The Period of *Détente*, 1963–79

> **KEY ISSUE** To what extent had the Cold War in Europe changed its character by 1973?

In the 1960s both the USSR and USA wanted a relaxation of tension in Europe. The USA was distracted by the Vietnam War, while the USSR faced serious economic problems and a growing challenge from China. This resulted in the Test Ban Treaty of 1963 and the Agreement on the Non-Proliferation of Nuclear Weapons in 1969. The construction of the Berlin Wall had forced the FRG to rethink its relations with the GDR, as it now seemed that the latter would survive for the foreseeable future. Despite the invasion of Czechoslovakia in August 1968 by Warsaw Pact forces to crush the 'Prague Spring' (the liberalisation process put into effect by Alexander Dubcek), Willy Brandt, the new Social Democratic Chancellor in Bonn, launched his Eastern Policy or *Ostpolitik* in October 1969. The FRG now recognised the GDR as a legal state and accepted the postwar frontiers of Poland and Czechoslovakia. Parallel to these negotiations the four victorious Powers of 1945 negotiated an agreement guaranteeing West Berlin's links with the FRG. Together with the Helsinki Conference on Security and Cooperation in 1975 these treaties did much to stabilise the situation in Eastern Europe, but Europe remained divided into two armed and potentially hostile blocs. By this date contemporaries believed that the division of Europe and the Cold War would last for an eternity, yet the strength of the USSR was less formidable than it seemed.

8 The Third or 'New Cold War' and the Collapse of Communism, 1979–91

> **KEY ISSUE** Why did the Cold War end?

What can be called a third or the 'New Cold War' was started by the USSR's decision to deploy a second generation of medium range nuclear missiles in Europe and to intervene in Afghanistan in December 1979. America and the Western Powers responded vigorously by deploying Cruise missiles in Western Europe. In 1983 President Reagan escalated the arms race in a dramatic way by announcing the Strategic Defence Initiative, which was a plan to enable the USA to destroy Soviet missiles launched into the atmosphere. Faced with this new and vastly expensive challenge, military defeat in Afghanistan, the flare up of ethnic conflicts at home and national bankruptcy, Mikhail Gorbachev, who came to power in 1985, had little option but to end the Cold War and seek Western loans to modernise the Soviet economy. Once it became clear in 1989 that the USSR would no longer prop up the satellite regimes in Eastern Europe, they collapsed like a house of cards. They failed to survive because they were kept in place by Soviet bayonets, were therefore by necessity police states and were unable to match Western Europe's prosperity.

9 The Nuclear Background

> **KEY ISSUE** What role did nuclear weapons play in the Cold War?

What prevented the Cold War from becoming a 'hot war' was the balance of terror created by nuclear weapons. When the USA dropped nuclear bombs on Hiroshima and Nagasaki, it was clear that a 'quantum jump'[14] in destructive weapons had been reached. Stalin responded by speeding up work on developing a Soviet atom bomb, which was tested on 20 August 1949. Both Powers then went on to develop hydrogen bombs, thermonuclear devices, which exploded at a very high temperature, and to design long range bombers that could carry them. Over the next decade bombers were replaced by rockets. Thanks to the assistance of German scientists, captured at the end of the Second World War, the Soviets successfully fired the world's first inter-continental missile (ICBM) in August 1957. Horrified by the apparent evidence of a missile gap, the USA first of all produced Thor and Jupiter missiles, and then went on to develop a whole new generation of rockets, which included the Polaris missiles that could be fired from submarines. Steadily over the next twenty-five years these lethal systems were expanded and improved

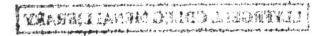

on. In sheer quantity of missiles the USSR caught up with the USA by the early 1970s. Computerised guidance systems could now accurately guide ICBMs to their targets while the development of MIRVs (multiple independently targeted re-entry vehicles) could fire well over twelve nuclear missiles on different targets. In any nuclear conflict it was inconceivable that there could be a winner. In 1980 what President Dwight Eisenhower had told the South Korean leader, Syngman Rhee, in 1953 was still valid:

> ... There will be millions of people dead. War today is unthinkable with the weapons which we have at our command. If the Kremlin and Washington ever lock up in a war, the results are too horrible to contemplate.

Only in 1983 did the American pioneered Strategic Defence Initiative achieve a revolutionary breakthrough, which challenged this doctrine of mutual assured destruction, or MAD. By planning to set up a protective shield of lasers and particle beam weapons in space aimed against ballistic missiles, it seemed that the USA might eventually become immune to soviet missile attacks. Whether this would really have been effective in the 1980s we do not know, but it certainly scared the Soviets into seeking a new *détente* and ultimately into ending the Cold War.

10 Basic Issues in the Cold War, 1945–91

> **KEY ISSUE** What are the basic questions an historian should ask about the Cold War?

To understand the complex events of the Cold War it is useful if you keep the following key questions in mind as you read through this book:

- How did the Cold War begin? Was it the result of the actions of one Power – the USA or USSR, or a more complex interaction of factors in which the lesser Powers, the vacuum created by the defeat of Hitler and mutual suspicion all played a part?
- What was the Cold War in Europe and why did it never become a 'hot' war?
- Why did the Cold War last so long?
- Was the collapse of Communism in Eastern Europe inevitable?

References

1 D. Reynolds, ed., *The Origins of the Cold War in Europe: International Perspectives* (Yale U.P., 1994), p. 234.
2 George Orwell, quoted in *ibid.*, p. 1.

3 John W. Mason, *The Cold War, 1945–91* (Routledge, 1996), p. 5.
4 Anders Stephanson quoted in Reynolds, *op.cit.,* p. 24.
5 *Ibid.,* pp. 1–2.
6 *Ibid.,* p. 57
7 H. Roffmann, *Understanding The Cold War* (Fairleigh Dickinson UP/ Associated Press, 1977), p. 10.
8 J.L. Gaddis, *We Know Now: Rethinking Cold War History* (OUP, 1997), p. 9.
9 Louis Halle quoted in Reynolds, *op.cit.,* p. 29
10 Gaddis, *op.cit.,* pp. 28–33.
11 W. A. Williams quoted in Reynolds *op.cit.,* p. 30.
12 Gabriel Kolko in *ibid.* p. 32.
13 *Ibid.,* p. 15.
14 Gaddis *op.cit.,* p. 86.

Summary Diagram
The Cold War in Europe, 1945–91: An Overview

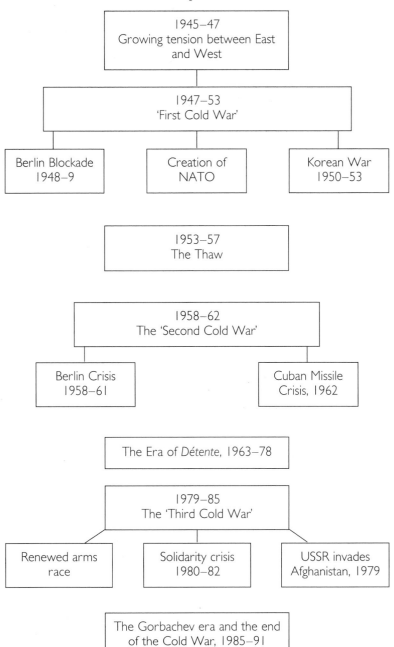

Working on Chapter I

This chapter provides an overview of the whole of the Cold War and its impact on Europe. Before moving on to the next chapter write out the time-line from page 1. Add to it to any further significant dates which you have found in Chapter 1. If possible, it would be a good idea to write out this list with the help of a computer or word processor so that you can add to it easily as you read on. Also, as far as you can at this stage, write out brief answers to the Key Issue questions.

Answering structured and essay questions on Chapter I

At the end of each chapter in this book there are structured and essay questions with advice on how to answer them. Here is some introductory information on how to cope with these two types of exam questions:

Structured questions usually require two different responses:

i. You will be asked to 'outline', which in fact means describe, a sequence of events. To gain full marks in this sort of question you need to know the facts and make sure that you cover the full range of *relevant* events.

ii. Then instead of outlining a sequence of events, you will be set a question which requires more thought, analysis and explanation. You might, for example, be asked to explain *why* a particular event occurred or *what* its consequences were.

You will also have to write essays on more wide ranging topics. A typical question could be:

Why was war between the USSR and the Western Powers averted in Europe in the period 1948–90?

When preparing an essay of this sort it would be a good idea to take the following steps:

● Ask yourself what are the key words. In this case they are: 'Why ... war averted between 1945 and 1990'.

● Then decide on the key themes of your answer and how you will effectively use them to answer the question. Here the key themes are the economic weakness of the USSR and the essentially defensive policies of Stalin, the American policy of containment, the nuclear balance and the gradual settling down of the Cold War in Europe into an uneasy balance of power after 1953. Remember that you must flesh this out with accurate evidence and not write it down in narrative form. You are required to construct an *argument* backed up with relevant evidence. Before you start writing the essay, it is a good idea to draw up a plan.

● Your essay should have a short introductory paragraph in which you introduce the gist of your main arguments.

- Then in the main section of your essay you should develop these arguments further and back them up with well chosen evidence.
- Most students find the final paragraph the most difficult. Just repeating points you have already made earlier in the essay in a more simplified form will not bring you any extra credit. It is better to end your essay with your strongest and most convincing argument, which reinforces those you have made elsewhere. Supported by a brief quotation or reference to a relevant historian, this can be a very effective way of rounding off your essay.

2 The Defeat of the Axis Powers, 1943–45: The Cold War Foreshadowed?

POINTS TO CONSIDER

This chapter will focus on the period 1943–45, which saw the defeat and occupation of Nazi Germany and the liberation of Continental Europe. Already by the winter of 1944/45 growing rivalry and mistrust were causing serious strains between Britain and the USA on the one side, and the USSR on the other. As you read through this chapter, you must ask yourself whether a break between the Anglo-Americans and the Soviets was inevitable by the Spring of 1945 or if a continuation of Great Power cooperation seemed the more likely.

KEY DATES

1943	3 Sept	Italian Armistice.
	28 Nov–1 Dec	Teheran Conference.
1944	6 June	Allied forces invade France.
	July	Red Army enters Central Poland; National Liberation Committee set up.
	23 Aug	Formation of coalition government in Romania.
	9 Sept	Communist coup in Bulgaria.
	9 Oct	Anglo-Soviet 'percentages agreement'.
	Dec	British suppress Communist uprising in Greece.
	10 Dec	Franco-Soviet treaty.
1945	4–11 Feb	Yalta Conference.
	Apr	Liberation of Czechoslovakia.
	8 May	Unconditional German surrender.

1 The Conflicting Aims of the Big Three

> **KEY ISSUES** To what extent did the individual aims of the Big Three Powers conflict and was this one of the basic causes of the Cold War?

All three members of the Grand Alliance were in agreement that Germany should never again be in a position to unleash a world war. They also hoped to continue the wartime alliance that had been so successful, but as victory over the Axis Powers became more certain, they began to develop their own often conflicting aims and agendas for postwar Europe.

a) The USSR

In the early 1950s most Western observers assumed that Moscow's main aim was to destroy the Western Powers and create global Communism, yet recent historical research, which the end of the Cold War has made possible, has shown that Stalin's policy was often more flexible and less ambitious than it appeared to be at the time. By the winter of 1944/5 his immediate priorities were clear. He wanted security for the USSR and reparations from Germany and its allies. To protect the USSR against any future German attack he was determined to hang on to the land annexed from Poland in 1939, and, as compensation, to give the Poles the German territories which lay beyond the river Oder. He also aimed to reintegrate into the USSR the Baltic provinces and territory, which had been lost to Finland in 1941, annex Besserabia and to bring both Romania and Bulgaria within the Soviet orbit (see map page 2). In Eastern Europe Stalin's first priority was to ensure that regimes friendly to the USSR were set up. In some states like Poland and Romania this could only be guaranteed by a Communist government, but in others, such as Hungary and Czecholsovakia, Stalin was prepared to tolerate more broadly based governments in which the Communists formed a minority. By 1944 Stalin seems to have envisaged a postwar Europe made up of three different areas:

● An area under direct Soviet control in Eastern Europe: Poland, Romania, Bulgaria and, for a time at least, the future Soviet zone in Germany;
● An intermediate zone comprising Yugoslavia, Austria, Hungary, Czechoslovakia and Finland, in which the Communists should share power with the middle class parties and form a bridge to the West;
● A non-Communist Western Europe, which would also include Greece.

b) The USA

In the 1950s Western historians, such as Herbert Feiss,[1] used to argue that USA was too preoccupied with winning the struggle against Nazi Germany and Japan to give much thought to the shape of postwar Europe, since it assumed that all problems would in due course be solved in cooperation with Britain and the USSR. Yet this view of the USA has been sharply criticized by the revisionist historians of the 1960s and 1970s. More recently Melvyn Leffler[2] has shown that the surprise Japanese attack on Pearl Harbor in 1941 and the dramatic developments in air technology during the war had made the Americans feel vulnerable to potential threats from foreign Powers. Consequently, as early as 1943–4, American officials began to draw up plans for a chain of bases, which would give the USA control of both the Pacific and Atlantic Ocean, and guarantee that American industry and trade would have access to the raw materials and markets of most of Western Europe and Asia. Much of Roosevelt's policy was inspired by the ideas of President Wilson, who in 1919 had hoped eventually to turn the world into one large free trade area, composed of democratic states, where tariffs and economic nationalism would be abolished. Washington was determined that there should be no more attempts by the Germans to create a self-sufficient or autarchic economy, and that the British and French, too, would have to abolish tariffs and allow other states to trade freely with their empires. These ideas were all embodied in the Atlantic Charter, which Churchill and Roosevelt drew up in August 1941. The new liberal world order was to be underpinned by the United Nations Organisation. By late 1943 Roosevelt envisaged this as being composed of an assembly where all the nations of the world would be represented, but real power and influence would be wielded by an executive committee, or Security Council, which would be dominated by the Big Three and China. For all his talk about Wilsonian Liberalism, he realised that the future of the postwar world would be decided by the Great Powers.

c) Great Britain

The British Government's main aim was to survive as an independent Great Power on friendly terms with both the USA and USSR, but it was alarmed by the prospect of Soviet influence spreading into Central Europe and the Eastern Mediterranean where it had vital strategic and economic interests. As Britain had gone to war over Poland, Churchill also wanted to see a democratic government in Warsaw, even though he conceded that its Eastern frontiers would have to be altered in favour of the USSR.

2 Inter-Allied Negotiations, 1943–44

> **KEY ISSUE** How far had the Great Powers agreed on dividing up Europe into spheres of influence by the end of 1944?

In the Autumn of 1943 the foreign ministers of the Big Three met for the first time together in Moscow in an effort to reconcile their conflicting ambitions for postwar Europe. They agreed to set up the European Advisory Commission to finalise plans for the postwar Allied occupation of Germany and also to a joint Declaration on General Security, which proposed the creation of an international organisation (or United Nations) for maintaining global peace and security. This would be joined by all the 'peace loving states'. Publicly the Americans argued that a United Nations organisation would make unnecessary any Soviet or British plans for creating spheres of influence to defend their interests. However, at the conference at Tehran in November 1943, attended by Churchill, Roosevelt and Stalin, the decision to land British and American troops in France rather than in the Balkans effectively ensured that the USSR would liberate both Eastern and South-Eastern Europe by itself and hence be in a position to turn the whole region into a Soviet sphere of influence. It was this factor that left Churchill and Roosevelt with little option but to recognise the USSR's claims to Eastern Poland.

A year later, in an effort to protect British interests in the Eastern Mediterranean, Churchill flew to Moscow and proposed dividing South Eastern Europe up into distinct zones of interest. This formed the basis of the notorious percentages agreement, which Churchill wrote out 'on a half sheet of paper' as follows:

Rumania	
Russia	**90%**
The others	**10%**
Greece	
Great Britain	**90%**
(in accord with the USA)	
Russia	**10%**
Yugoslavia	**50–50%**
Hungary	**50–50%**
Bulgaria	
Russia	**75%**
The others	**25%**

(Yugoslavia and Hungary were to be divided equally into British and Russian zones of interest.)

Stalin approved the proposal but the following day Molotov, his Foreign Minister, attempted to revise the percentages in Hungary and Bulgaria in favour of the USSR when he demanded a 75 per cent Soviet say in the former and 90 per cent in the latter. The agreement was therefore never confirmed but it broadly corresponded to initial Soviet intentions in Eastern Europe. It was, however, rejected outright by Roosevelt, who informed Stalin that there was 'in this global war . . . no question, either military or political, in which the United States [was] not interested'. This may have been, as Yergin has pointed out, 'a fundamental statement of the new global vision that would shape American policy in the postwar era',[3] but with the Red Army advancing steadily towards the River Oder, there was little Roosevelt could do to stop Stalin from turning all of Eastern Europe into a Soviet sphere of interest.

POLAND'S FRONTIERS

In 1919 when modern Poland was set up by the Treaty of Versailles, the British Foreign Minister, Lord Curzon, proposed that its frontier with Russia should run about 100 miles to the East of Warsaw (the so-called Curzon line), but the Poles rejected this, and in early 1920, exploiting the chaos of the Russian Civil War, invaded the Ukraine. By the Treaty of Riga in 1921 they annexed a considerable amount of the Western Russian border territories (see map page 2). In 1939, as a result of the Nazi–Soviet Pact, the USSR regained these territories when Hitler defeated Poland in September, but lost them again after the German invasion of the Soviet Union in June 1941. Stalin remained determined to reclaim them at the end of the War.

3 The Liberation of Europe, 1943–45

KEY ISSUES In what ways was the future of Continental Europe decided in 1944–45 by the way it was liberated? Was Europe already in June 1945 effectively divided into two blocs?

The liberation of Eastern Europe by Soviet forces and Western Europe by predominantly Anglo-American armies created the context for the Cold War. To understand the complex political situation created by the liberation it is important to remember the following factors as you read through the next section:

- Bulgaria, Finland, Italy, Hungary and Romania were Axis states, that is allies of Germany. Although they were allowed their own governments after their occupation, real power rested with the Allied Control Commissions (ACC). The first ACC was set up in Southern Italy in 1943 by the British and Americans after the collapse of Fascism. As the USSR had no troops in Italy, it was not represented on it. Similarly, as it was the USSR that had liberated Eastern Europe, Soviet officials dominated the ACCs in Romania, Bulgaria, Finland and Hungary. In this respect Soviet policy was the 'mirror image' of Anglo-American policy in Italy.
- In the states actually occupied by the Germans and Italians in Eastern and South-Eastern Europe (Poland, Czechoslovakia, Greece, and Yugoslavia) governments-in-exile were set up in London. They were made up of representatives of the prewar parties, who had managed to escape occupation, yet, being in London, they lost control of the partisan (guerrilla) groups fighting in the occupied territories. Except for Poland the Communist

partisan groups emerged as the strongest local forces and their leaders were not ready to take orders from their governments-in-exile. Sometimes this suited Stalin, and sometimes, as in Greece, it did not.

● In the liberated territories Stalin advised the local Communists parties to form popular fronts or alliances with the Liberal, Socialist and Peasant parties. Eventually these fronts became the means by which Communism seized power in Eastern Europe.

a) Poland

The Polish question was one of the most complex problems facing the Allies. Britain and France had gone to war in the first instance to preserve Polish independence, while the USSR in 1939 had profited from the German rape of Poland to annex its Eastern territories. It was determined not only to regain these lands, but also to ensure that there was a friendly government in Warsaw. Inevitably this aim made the Soviet Union 'enemy number two'[4] to all Poles, except the Communists, and in turn ensured that Stalin initially treated Poland as an occupied territory and liquidated the resistance groups hostile to him. Consequently, long before the Soviet 'liberation' of Poland, Stalin took the necessary precautions to ensure that no independent government hostile to the USSR would ever gain power in Warsaw. In 1940 he ordered 4,000 Polish officers to be shot at Katyn, near Smolensk, while a few months later the Russian Secret Police, the NKVD, began training Polish volunteers to form a similar service in Poland. Once the Red Army crossed the Polish frontier in early January 1944, Stalin systematically destroyed the non-Communist resistance, the Polish Home Army, but did not allow the Polish Communists to seize power straight away for fear of antagonising the Western Powers.

In July he fatally undermined the authority of the Polish Government-in-exile by setting up the Committee of National Liberation, which he considered to be the core of a future Polish administration. Its role was to camouflage the extent of Communist control in Poland by appealing to a wide cross-section of society which wanted social reform. It had to reassure both the Western Governments and the Poles themselves that the USSR had no immediate intention of creating a Communist Poland. Stalin continued this dual strategy with some success. The Western Powers clung to the hope that Stalin would not insist on a Communist regime provided he received territorial concessions in Eastern Poland.

His real policy was revealed when the underground Polish Home Army rose up in revolt against the Germans in Warsaw in August 1944 and made a desperate attempt to seize the initiative before the Red Army could overrun the whole of Poland. By gaining control of Warsaw the Home Army hoped that it would win the backing of the Western Allies and so thwart Stalin's policy in Poland. Although Soviet troops penetrated to within 12 miles of Warsaw, the Polish insurgents were left to fight it out alone with the Germans, who finally defeated them on 2 October. Stalin refused to grant American requests for permission to land and refuel planes carrying supplies for the rebels until mid September by which time it was too late for them to make any difference. In this way he managed to ensure that the most active political opponents of Communism were eliminated, and inevitably this made it easier for him to enforce his policy in Poland. As Soviet troops moved further West towards the river Oder in the remaining months of 1944, the NKVD, assisted by Polish Communists, shot or imprisoned thousands of partisans from the Home Army.

Despite all that had happened, Roosevelt still clung to the hope that, once the United Nations Organisation was set up, it would be possible to reach a compromise with Stalin about the future of Poland. He was determined to avoid a premature break with the USSR over the Polish question. Consequently when the Soviets formally recognised in January 1945 the Communist dominated Committee for National Liberation as the provisional government of Poland, Britain and the USA, even though they supported the Polish Government-in-exile in London, played down the significance of what the Soviets had done in the interests of Great Power unity.

b) Romania and Bulgaria

On August 20 1944 the Soviets launched a major offensive to drive the German army out of the Balkans. The immediate consequences of this brought about the collapse of the pro-German regimes in both Romania and Bulgaria. Like Poland, both states were vital to the security of the USSR. As an American intelligence report pointed out in 1946,

1 Military control of Rumania [sic] gives the Soviet union ready access to
   the land routes into Yugoslavia, Bulgaria and Central Europe, as well as
   domination of the Danube river and increased control over the Black
   Sea ... Soviet control of Bulgaria provides the Soviet Union with an
5 advance base dominating the approaches to the Turkish Straits and the
   Greek frontier .... [see map page 2]

Russia was also determined to re-annex the former Romanian territories of Besserabia and Northern Bukovina, which it had occupied in 1940. In a desperate attempt to seize the initiative before the Soviets arrived, the Romanian King deposed the pro-Nazi dictator, Marshal Antonescu. He was supported by the Liberal and non-Socialist parties, who hoped that, like Italy, Romania would be able to negotiate a ceasefire with the Western Allies and form a government in which the Communists would be in a minority. This idea was an illusion based on the false assumption that the British would open up a second front in the Balkans. In reality the King had no alternative except to surrender to the Russians.

The British and American ambassadors already tacitly accepted that

Romania was a Soviet sphere of influence, and gave no help to the Romanian delegation, which was particularly anxious to obtain a guarantee that Soviet troops would be withdrawn as soon as the war with Germany was over. An Allied Control Commission was set up, which was dominated by Soviet officials. A coalition Government composed of Communists, Socialists, Liberals and the left-wing peasants' party, the Ploughmen's Front, was formed, but, backed by Soviet officials on the ACC, the Communists and their allies in the winter of 1944/45 made Romania ungovernable. They formed the National Democratic Front and incited the peasants to seize farms from the landowners and the workers to set up Communist-dominated production committees in the factories. In March 1945 Stalin, following the precedent set by the British, who had intervened in December 1945 in Greece (see page 25), orchestrated a coup which led to the creation of the Communist dominated National Democratic Front Government.

Although Stalin did not want a break with the West, Western observers nevertheless noted the essentially anti-western thrust of Soviet policy in Romania. One American official observed in November 1944, for example, that

 1 Soviet policy in Rumania [*sic*] tends towards weakening the position of
   the bourgeois [middle] class. Western influences are deeply rooted in
   the bourgeoisie and consequently they feel less favourable towards
   Russia. The Russians prefer the weight of political decision to be with
 5 the peasant and working classes which are not permeated [penetrated]
   with Western ideology.

The collapse of Romania at the end of August 1944 gave Stalin the opportunity to occupy Bulgaria, which was technically at war with Britain and the USA, but not with the USSR. On 8 September the Red Army crossed the frontier. The local Communists controlled several thousand armed partisans, and in 1942 had set up a 'Patriotic Front' composed of the Social Democrats, left-wing Agrarians and members of Zveno, a group of anti-royalist officers. The Front, with the Communists playing a key role, seized power and set up a government in Sofia shortly before the Red Army arrived. Inevitably this success strengthened the local Communists, who attempted immediately to implement a Communist revolution in Bulgaria. The country's former ruling class were purged and well over 10,000 people executed. The trade unions and police were infiltrated and the large farms were taken over by peasant cooperatives.

This enthusiasm for revolution did not, however, fit in with Stalin's overall strategy. Essentially he was determined to safeguard Soviet control over Bulgaria, yet not antagonise his Western allies any more than necessary while the war with Germany was still being fought, and at a time when Poland was becoming an increasingly divisive issue. Since the USSR's position was guaranteed through the key role of the Soviet chairman of the ACC, and the strong position of the local

Communist party, Stalin attempted in the Autumn of 1944 to per-suade the Bulgarian Communists to pursue a more moderate policy. He wanted them to tolerate a certain degree of political opposition and to work within the Patriotic Front coalition, but this policy was not easy to carry out, as the local Communists, sometimes backed by Soviet officials on the ACC, were determined to gain complete power regardless of the diplomatic consequences.

c) Yugoslavia

After the occupation of Bulgaria Soviet troops linked up with Yugoslav partisan forces under the Communist leader, Joseph Tito, and launched an attack on Belgrade on 14 October. By this time Tito was a formidable ally. He had built up an effective partisan army, which not only fought the Germans but also waged civil war against the Serbian Nationalist leader, Colonel Mihailovic. As soon as his parti-sans occupied an area, they formed Communist dominated liberation committees, which took their orders from him rather than the Yugoslav Government-in-exile in London. Tito's position was enor-mously strengthened when the British decided for military reasons in May 1944 to assist him rather than Mihailovic.

To the Soviets the key to controlling the situation in South-Eastern Europe was to build up a military and political alliance between Yugoslavia, Bulgaria and the USSR. Molotov told Tito in April 1944 that he wanted Yugoslavia to become 'our chief mainstay in South East Europe'.[5] Up to 1948 Tito was certainly a loyal ally of Stalin, but he still tried to carry out his own policies independently of the USSR. Despite Stalin's fear of provoking the Western powers, Tito did not abandon his plans for introducing Communist regimes into Yugoslavia and Albania, which his forces had also liberated in November 1944. Stalin was, however, able to exercise a firmer control over his foreign policy. In January 1945, he vetoed his scheme for a federation with Bulgaria, which would have turned the latter state into a mere province of Yugoslavia. He made it very clear that Yugoslavia would have to subordinate its local territorial ambitions to the overall foreign policy considerations determined by Moscow.

d) Greece

Tito and Stalin also clashed over the attempts by the Communist con-trolled People's Liberation Army (*Elas*) in Greece to set up a National Liberation Government on the Yugoslav model. During the War *Elas* had emerged as the most effective resistance force in Greece, and, like Tito's partisans, had fought the Germans, whilst also attempting to eliminate rival non-Communist guerrilla groups. A British his-torian, C.M. Woodhouse, has observed that in Greece 'as early as 1942 one of two consequences was already inevitable: either a civil war or an unopposed Communist take-over'.[6] Yet as Greece was an area regarded by Stalin as being well within the British sphere of influence, he urged *Elas* to join a moderate coalition government. When the British forces in Greece ordered Elas to disband its partisan force, a revolt, encouraged by Tito, broke out in Athens on 3 December. Stalin, true to his agreement with Churchill (see page 19), stopped Tito from helping the Greek Communists and raised no objection to their defeat by British troops.

e) Hungary and Czechoslovakia

In neither Czechoslovakia nor Hungary did Stalin have any immediate plans for a Communist seizure of power, as he was anxious to avoid provoking trouble with Britain and the USA, while he consolidated his position in Poland. The local Communist parties were consequently ordered to enter democratic coalition governments and to work from within to consolidate their position.

i) Hungary

In 1943 the Hungarians secretly attempted to negotiate an armistice with Britain and America, so that they could be spared liberation by Soviet troops, but the decision not to open up a second front in the Balkans ensured Hungary's fate would be decided by the Red Army. When Soviet troops crossed the Hungarian frontier in September 1944, Admiral Horthy, the head of state, appealed to the Soviets for a ceasefire, but the Germans took Horthy prisoner and encouraged the Hungarian Nazis, the Arrow Cross Party, to seize power in Western Hungary. It was not until early December 1944 that Red Army units reached the outskirts of Budapest.

In the Soviet occupied section of the country the Communist party was at first too weak to play a dominant role in politics, and it therefore had little option but to cooperate with the Social Democrats, the Smallholders (a peasants' party) and several other middle class parties. In December 1945, when elections took place for the National Assembly, the Communists, despite the presence of the Red Army, only gained some 17 per cent of the votes cast, but they were given three key posts in the Provisional National Government. Throughout 1945 Stalin's immediate aim was to strip Hungary completely bare of anything that could be taken to the USSR as reparations. In the longer term he was not sure whether to integrate Hungary into the Soviet bloc or allow it the necessary independence to act as a bridge between Eastern and Western Europe.

ii) Czechoslovakia

Of all the Eastern European states Czechoslovakia was the closest to the USSR. The Czechs felt betrayed by Britain and France over the

Munich settlement of 1938, which had awarded the Sudetenland to Germany, and looked to the USSR as the Power that would restore their country's pre-1938 borders. In 1943 the Czech Government-in-exile under Benes negotiated an alliance with the USSR, although this still did not stop Stalin from annexing Ruthenia in the Autumn of 1944 (see map page 2).

As the Soviet army occupied more and more of Czechoslovakia in the winter of 1944–45 the balance of power tilted steadily away from the democratic parties represented by the Government-in-exile in London to the Czech Communist Party led by Gottwald who was in Moscow. Stalin nevertheless forced Gottwald to accept Benes as President and work within a coalition government. In turn, Benes followed a conciliatory policy, which enabled Stalin to achieve a harmony that had been impossible to reach in Poland. In January 1945 the London and the Communist political leaders met in Moscow. In retrospect Rudolf Slansky, the Communist Party Secretary, wrote that 'here for the first time there was joined the battle of two political worlds'.[7] Yet Benes, as the future constitutional President of Czechslovakia, refused to take sides against the Communists. When the Provisional Government was formed, the Communists were able to demand eight seats in the cabinet including the influential Ministries of the Interior and Information, although Gottwald skilfully camouflaged their powerful position by not claiming the premiership.

f) Finland

Finland had been part of the Russian empire up to 1917. In early 1940 it had been defeated by Soviet forces after the brief Winter War, and in 1941, not surprisingly, supported the Nazi attack on the USSR. Yet despite this record, in the Summer of 1944, when Soviet troops invaded Finland, the Finns were granted an armistice on unexpectedly generous terms. They had to declare war on the Germans, eventually cede part of the strategically important Petsamo region (see map page 2) on the Arctic coast to the USSR and pay reparations, but politically they were allowed a considerable degree of freedom. Marshal Mannerheim, who had cooperated closely with Hitler, remained president until 1946 and there was only one Communist in the first postwar cabinet.

Why did Stalin pursue such a moderate policy in Finland? To a certain extent this fitted in with his policy of 'ideological *détente*' which he had followed since the dissolution in 1943 of the Comintern, the Communist International Organisation based in Moscow. This was a gesture aimed at Britain and the USA to convince them that the USSR was no longer planning world revolution. At this stage Stalin appeared to believe that each state would find its own way to Socialism in its own time. The Finns, unlike the Hungarians, were also lucky enough to be able to quit the war at the right moment and were in a position to give the USSR such vitally needed reparations as barges, rolling stock and manufactured goods. A repressive occupation policy would have disrupted these deliveries.

g) The Liberation of France and Italy

Italy and France were liberated by the Western Powers. Italy was a leading Axis state, while France until its defeat in 1940 had played the main part in the war against Germany. In both states resistance to the Germans and the Fascist authorities 'legitimised' or made respectable the Communist party.

i) Italy

It took nearly two years to liberate Italy. After the Allied landings in Sicily in July 1943 Mussolini was overthrown and in September an armistice was signed, but Allied forces were unable to stop the Germans seizing Rome. They were then forced to fight their way up the peninsular, and it was only in April 1945 that Northern Italy was at last liberated. Italy was the first enemy state to sign an armistice, and the way its occupied areas were administered set important precedents for the future. All Soviet requests to be involved were firmly rejected by the British and Americans, which later gave Stalin an excuse to exclude them from Eastern Europe. An Italian government was set up, and gradually it was given responsibility for the liberated areas, although it was closely supervised by the Anglo-American Allied Control Commission. Large areas behind the front continued to be under the direct control of the Allied Commander-in-Chief. Stalin had little option but to accept these arrangements, although he was determined that the Italian Communists should not be excluded from participating in government. Ignoring the fact that Italy's external relations were controlled by the Western Allies, Stalin went ahead on 14 March 1944, and officially recognised the Italian government. A few days earlier he had given Palmiro Togliatti, the leader of the Italian Communist Party, a 'plan of action', according to which he was to form a coalition with the Socialists. He was to avoid any premature mass action, such as an uprising or civil war, which would cause acute tension between the USSR and the West and so make it more difficult for Stalin to consolidate his position in Eastern Europe. He was also to draft a popular programme for reforming the Italian economy, which would prepare the way for later Communist electoral successes.

Togliatti carried out these instructions as well as he could. He joined the new government which was formed when Rome fell in June 1944. In the north in the winter of 1944/45 the Communists played a key role in the resistance against the Germans. Togliatti, only too aware of how the British had crushed the Greek revolt, managed to keep his more radical partisans in check. By the time the war had ended, the resistance had, as Martin Clark has written, '"legitimized" the PCI [Italian Communist party] and made it an indispensable pillar of the new national unity'.[8] This was seen when Togliatti himself became Minister of Justice in the Italian government, which was formed in April 1945.

ii) France

When Paris was liberated in August 1944, General de Gaulle, the leader of the Free French, immediately established an independent government. His aim was to rebuild French power and to create a powerful French led Western European bloc. To counter the predominance of the Anglo-Americans he looked to Russia, and in December 1944 signed the Franco-Soviet Treaty, which actually committed France to supporting the USSR, if in the future it should have to launch a preventive war against Germany.

As in Italy the French Communist Party, having played a prominent part in the Resistance, became a major force in French politics. Its leader, Maurice Thorez, was instructed by Stalin to support the Soviet-French alliance and work towards creating a left-wing coalition with the Socialists, which, it was hoped, would eventually be able to form a government.

4 The Yalta Conference, February 1945

KEY ISSUE What was achieved at Yalta?

The Yalta Conference, attended by Churchill, Roosevelt and Stalin, was 'the last of the wartime conferences ... [and] the first of the postwar summits'.[9] Besides drawing up plans for finishing the war in Europe and the Far East, it also attempted to lay the foundations of the coming peace. Plans were finalised for the occupation of Germany by the victorious powers, amongst whom on Churchill's insistence, France was to be included (see map page 38). Each was allotted their own zone, including a section of Berlin, which was placed under Four Power control. The decision was taken to set up the United Nations. Poland again proved to be the most difficult subject on the agenda, and the Allies were only able to reach agreement through a series of ambiguous compromises, which could be read differently by the USSR and the Western Powers:

- Poland's Eastern border would run along the Curzon line (see page 20), and as compensation for the land lost to the Soviet Union, it would receive a substantial increase in territory in the North and West. The exact details of this were not stated.
- The decision was also taken to reorganise the Provisional Government by including democratic politicians both from Poland and the London Government-in-exile.

- Elections would be held as soon as possible.

Superficially this seemed to be a success for the British and Americans, but in fact the terms were so vague that Stalin could easily manipulate them. In the words of the American Chief of Staff, Admiral Leahy, the Soviets could stretch the agreement 'all the way from Yalta to Washington without ever technically breaking it'.[10]

To underpin the right of the liberated states to determine their own governments Roosevelt persuaded Stalin and Churchill to agree to the Declaration on Liberated Europe, which committed the three governments to:

> 1 jointly assist the people in any European liberated state or former Axis
>   satellite state in Europe where in their judgment conditions require [sic]
>   (a) to establish conditions of internal peace (b) to carry out emergency
>   measures for the relief of distressed peoples; (c) to form interim gov-
> 5 ernmental authorities broadly representative of all democratic elements
>   in the population and pledged to the earliest possible establishment
>   through free elections of governments responsive to the will of the
>   people; and (d) to facilitate where necessary the holding of such elections.

Once the Cold War started, this became, as Martin Walker observed, a key text 'upon which all future accusations of Soviet betrayal and bad faith were made.'[11] Yet it completely ignored the reality of the situation in Eastern Europe. Stalin saw Poland as a corridor for an attack from Germany or Western Europe on the USSR. He was therefore going to ensure that a friendly government, which in Poland's case could only mean a Communist one, was in place.

5 The End of the War in Europe

> **KEY ISSUE** Why did Churchill view the USSR's advance westwards with suspicion?

Three months after the Yalta Conference the War in Europe ended, and East and West confronted each other in the vacuum caused by the defeat of the Axis powers. In the final weeks of the war there had been considerable jockeying for position by the Great Powers. British and American forces raced to Trieste in an attempt to stop Tito seizing the port, while the British army in North Germany crossed the Elbe and advanced into Mecklenburg to prevent the Soviets from occupying Denmark. Churchill also urged the Americans to make special efforts to take Berlin and Prague. He telegraphed to Truman, who had become President after Roosevelt had died on 12 April, that

> There can be little doubt that the liberation of Prague and as much as
> possible of the territory of Western Czechoslovakia by your forces
> might make the whole difference to the post-war situation in
> Czechoslovakia and might well influence that in nearby countries.

But the American generals were not ready to see their soldiers killed for what they regarded as political reasons, and so both capitals fell to Soviet troops. Nevertheless when the war ended with the surrender of Germany on 8 May 1945, Anglo-American forces occupied nearly half the area that was to become the Soviet Zone in Germany (see map page 38). It was not until early July that these troops were withdrawn into the American and British Zones.

6 Assessment

> **KEY ISSUES** Was Europe effectively divided into two blocs by 1945? Did the Cold War already seem inevitable?

The collapse of Germany and its allies had created a vacuum in Central Europe, which was filled by the advancing armies of the Grand Alliance. This created the context in which the Cold War was waged, but did it make the struggle inevitable? In many ways Stalin had shown himself to be pragmatic. He believed firmly in zones of influence. Provided that Soviet power was secure in the key states of Poland, Romania and Bulgaria, he was ready, at least for a time, to be flexible in Hungary, Finland and Czechoslovakia and respect the interests of his allies elsewhere, as his attitude to British intervention in Greece showed. In Italy and France he kept his options open by instructing the Communist Parties to join democratic coalitions. Roosevelt and Churchill privately conceded that Eastern Europe was predominantly a Soviet sphere of interest, and in practice treated Western Europe, particularly Italy, as an Anglo-American sphere of interest from which Soviet influence was excluded. They hoped that Stalin would eventually tolerate democratic governments in Eastern Europe and respect the *Declaration on Liberated Europe*. They accepted that the USSR had special interests in Poland, but it was Stalin's ruthless defence of these that already by the summer of 1945 had begun to alienate the West and make the *Declaration* a mockery.

References

1 H. Feiss, *Churchill–Roosevelt–Stalin* (Princeton, 1953).
2 M. Leffler, 'National Security and US Foreign Policy' in M. Leffler and D. Painter (ed.), *Origins of the Cold War* (Routledge, 1994), pp. 15–53.
3 D. Yergin, *Shattered Peace* (Houghton Miflin, 1977), p. 61.
4 K. Kersten, *The Establishment of Communist Rule in Poland, 1943–48* (University of California Press, 1991), p. 29.
5 V. Volkov, 'The Soviet Leadership and South Eastern Europe' in N. Naimark and L. Gibianskii, ed., *The Establishment of Communist Regimes in Eastern Europe, 1944–49* (Westview Press/HarperCollins, 1997), p. 56.
6 C.M. Woodhouse, *The Story of Modern Greece* (Faber and Faber, 1968), p. 248.
7 R. Luza, 'Czechoslovakia between Democracy and Communism' in C.M.

Maier (ed.), *The Cold War in Europe* (Markus Wiener, Princeton, 1996), p. 80.

8 M. Clark, *Modern Italy, 1871–1982* (Longman, 1984), p. 315.
9 M. Walker, *The Cold War* (Vintage, 1994), p. 13.
10 Quoted in Kersten, *op.cit.*, p. 123.
11 Walker, *op.cit.*, p. 14.

Summary Diagram
The Liberation of Europe, 1944–45

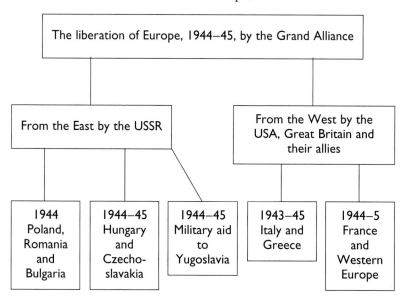

Working on Chapter 2

When writing up your notes avoid becoming bogged down in too much detail and concentrate on grasping the following key points:

- What were the aims of the Great Powers? To what extent did these clash?
- What was Stalin's policy towards the Eastern European states?
- Why was Poland such an important issue?
- To what extent were Anglo-American policies in Western Europe and the Eastern Mediterranean the mirror image of Soviet policies in Eastern Europe?

Answering structured and essay questions on Chapter 2

In this chapter you have looked at how the defeat of Germany and the Axis states brought the USSR and the Western Powers face to face and created the context for (some historians would say the cause of) the

Cold War. To understand the Cold War it is important for you to have a good basic knowledge of these complex events. Look at the following structured questions:

1. **a)** Outline the different policies adopted by Stalin for the states liberated by the USSR, 1943–45.
    b) To what extent were these policies hostile to the West?
2. **a)** What was Anglo-American policy towards Italy and the Eastern Mediterranean, 1943–45?
    b) Can this policy be described as 'the mirror image' of Soviet policy in Eastern Europe?

The most important words in question 1a) are 'outline the different policies'. You must therefore deal with each of the states in turn showing how 'differentiated' Stalin's policies in fact were. Question 1b) is more difficult because you have to analyse, compare and make judgements. First you must define what hostile means. Was Stalin consolidating Eastern Europe in order to overrun Western Europe after the War or was he acting defensively? Was his complete disregard for human life and liberties in Poland a challenge to the liberal values of the West? Why was he so lenient towards Hungary, Czechoslovakia and Finland, and why did he stop Tito intervening in Greece? Did he in fact want to remain on good terms with Britain and the USA after the War?

Only through analysis of what really happened can you answer these questions. Question 2a) requires less detail. In Italy you need to focus on why Britain and America excluded the USSR from participating in the Allied Military Government in 1943–45, while the key question in the Eastern Mediterranean is British policy towards Greece. Question 2b) requires more thought. Ask yourself what it is really getting at? Essentially it is asking you to look at whether Western Europe, particularly Italy, and the Eastern Mediterranean were in effect American and British spheres of influence from which the USSR was excluded. Was this really so different from Soviet policy in Poland, or at least Czechoslovakia, Hungary and Finland?

In essay questions you will need to employ a similar analytical technique, but they are more likely to be both more wide ranging and intellectually more challenging. Consider these questions, for example:

1. How serious were the divisions in the Grand Alliance in the period 1943–June 1945?
2. 'Only a desire to defeat Hitler kept the Grand Alliance united until the end of the War in Europe'. Discuss.
3. How true is it to say that for the cause of the Cold War the historian need look no further than the liberation of Europe?
4. 'Stalin showed a surprising pragmatism and readiness to compromise in seeking to secure Soviet interests in Europe in the period 1943–June 1945'. Discuss.

You will probably find question 1 the most straightforward. You must, of course, explore how divided the Alliance was, but the word 'how' also requires you to consider whether these divisions were in fact 'serious'. What does 'serious' mean? Of course there was friction, but was it 'serious' enough to break up the alliance once Nazi Germany was defeated? This is the point that question 3 is asking you to explore more specifically. Questions 2 and 4 both contain quotations. Here the examiner is challenging you to consider a particular view, which may be biased and only half-true. It will be your task in your essay to consider how accurate an interpretation the quotation is, and to show where it is ignoring or exaggerating the evidence. Do not feel that you have to agree with the point of view expressed. On the other hand, if you find it accurate, you must fully explain why.

Source-based questions on Chapter 2

The first and most essential skill in dealing with source-based questions is to make sure that you understand the context and background of the documents and technical terms used in them. The best way of making sure that you can do this is to know and understand thoroughly the period of history from which the sources are drawn.

1 Spheres of Influence in South Eastern Europe
Look carefully at the Churchill–Stalin percentages agreement on page 19, the American intelligence report on page 22 and the map on page 2.

a) Explain the following terms:
    i) 'military control' (page 22, line 1) (*3 marks*)
    ii) 'advance base' (page 22, line 5). (*2 marks*)
b) How far do the extracts explain Stalin's interest in Romania and Bulgaria? (7 marks)
c) To what extent was the Churchill-Stalin percentages agreement actually carried out in the period October 1944–May 1945? (*8 marks*)

2 The Liberation of Eastern Europe
Carefully read the extract on page 23 and the first extract on page 29.

a) Explain the following:
    i) 'Western influences are deeply rooted in the bourgeoisie' (page 23, lines 2–3) (*3 marks*)
    ii) 'former Axis satellite state' (page 29, lines 1–2). (*2 marks*)
b) What is the significance of point (c) in the Declaration on Liberated Europe (page 29, lines 4–8)? (*5 marks*)
c) In what ways is the American official in his report (on page 23) arguing that Soviet policy in Romania is essentially anti-Western? (*5 marks*)
d) Using both these extracts and your own knowledge explain why the Declaration on Liberated Europe ignored the reality of the situation in February 1945. (*10 marks*)

3 The Break-Up of the Grand Alliance, 1945–47

POINTS TO CONSIDER

This chapter will examine the reasons for the break up of the Grand Alliance between 1945 and 1947, and its consequences for Germany and Europe as a whole. It is important not only to understand the impact of Stalin's policies on Eastern Europe and of British, American and French policies on Western Europe, but also how the they interacted and increasingly began to tear the Continent apart.

KEY DATES

1945	July–Aug	Potsdam Conference.
1946	5 Mar	Churchill's Iron Curtain speech.
	21 Apr	Social Unity Party (SED) formed.
	Apr–July	Paris Conference of Foreign Ministers.
	3 May	General Clay halts reparation payments from Soviet Zone.
1947	1 Jan	Anglo-US Bizone formed.
	10 Feb	Peace treaties signed with Italy, Romania, Bulgaria, Finland and Hungary.
	12 Mar	Truman Doctrine announced.
	10 Mar–24 Apr	Council of Foreign Ministers' Meeting in Moscow.
	May	Communists excluded from government in France and Italy.
	5 June	Marshall Aid Programme announced.
	5 Oct	Cominform founded.

All three Great Powers wished to continue the wartime alliance, yet for an alliance to survive there needs to be either a common danger or agreement between its members on key principles. In postwar Europe this was no longer the case. Roosevelt had privately recognised that the West had little option but to accept Soviet control over Eastern Europe, but on his death in April 1945 he was replaced by Harry Truman, who was at first determined not to write it off as a Soviet sphere of interest and to pursue a much tougher policy towards the USSR. Not only did he strongly criticise Soviet policy in Poland, but in May he abruptly ended the lend-lease aid programme, which had made available food and armaments to the USSR during the war.

'Christmas Card' 1945 by the Egyptian cartoonist Kimon Marengo. It shows Truman (as the Statue of Liberty) with Stalin, Attlee, De Gaulle and Chiang Kai-shek.

1 The Potsdam Conference

> **KEY ISSUE** To what extent did the Potsdam Conference reveal fundamental disagreements between the wartime allies?

The inter-linked questions of Germany and Poland dominated the agenda of the Conference. Failure was only avoided by ambiguous compromises on all the most difficult issues. The Council of Foreign Ministers of the four Powers occupying Germany was set up in the hope that it would later deal with the difficult task of drawing up peace treaties with Germany and the Axis states. While Britain, the USA and USSR could agree on the necessary measures for German demilitarisation, denazification and the punishment of war criminals, they were only able to draw up the following minimal political and economic guidelines for the future of Germany:

- As there was no central German Government, an Allied Control Council was set up on which the Commanders-in-Chief of the armies of the four occupying Powers would sit. To avoid being outvoted by the three Western Powers, the Russians insisted that each commander should have complete responsibility for his own zone. This decision effectively stopped the Control Council from exercising any real power in Germany.
- A limited number of central German administrative departments dealing with finance, transport, trade and industry were to be formed at some point in the future.
- There was no agreement on how much reparations the USSR should be paid. The Soviets had already begun to strip their zone of industrial plant and raw materials, but the British and Americans were convinced that the German economy must be left sufficiently strong to pay for imported food and raw materials, and were not ready to subsidise the Soviet Zone. A compromise was negotiated whereby both the USSR and the Western Powers would take reparations from their own zones. In addition to this the British and Americans would grant 10 per cent of these to the Soviets and a further 15 per cent in exchange for the supply of food and raw materials from the Soviet Zone. The lack of a common reparation policy was a major step in the partition of Germany, as it made agreement on a joint four power economic policy much more difficult to achieve.

The USSR had already handed over to Poland all of Lower Silesia up to the Western Oder-Neisse line. At first London and Washington insisted that the Polish border lay along the Eastern Neisse, but then on second thoughts they decided to recognise the Western Neisse line in the unrealistic hope that this concession would persuade Stalin to adopt a more liberal policies in Poland (see map page 38).

THE IMPACT OF THE ATOM BOMB

Churchill had hoped that the 'Big Three' would meet as soon as possible after the end of the war in Europe, but it was not until 16 July that the Potsdam Conference opened. It was delayed because Truman wished to wait until the atom bomb had been tested at Alamogordo in New Mexico. When this took place successfully on 16 July, he was told that the bomb had a much greater destructive potential than was expected and was ready for immediate use against Japan. The news produced some dramatic changes in American policy. The Americans no longer wanted the USSR to join in the war against Japan, as now it seemed likely that they would quickly defeat Japan by themselves. American officials also thought that the possession of the bomb would enable the USA to force Stalin to make concessions in Eastern Europe. Michael Smith argues that the two atom bombs, which were dropped on Hiroshima and Nagasarki in early August, were primarily intended to impress the USSR, since, thanks to the code breakers at Bletchley Park in Britain, the Allies already knew that Japan was ready to surrender.[1] Stalin, however, refused to be intimidated. On the contrary the news about the bomb made him both more suspicious of the USA and determined to make the USSR a nuclear power as soon as possible.

2 The Peace Treaties with Italy and the Minor Axis Powers

KEY ISSUE Why, despite worsening relations between the USSR and Britain and the USA, was it possible to negotiate the peace treaties with Italy and the minor Axis powers?

At Potsdam it had been agreed that the Council of Foreign ministers would draw up the peace treaties with Germany's allies. Arguments broke out almost immediately at the first session of the Council in September 1945. The Soviets pressed for a harsh peace with Italy, while the British and Americans argued that Italy, having broken with Germany in September 1944, deserved more lenient treatment. The USSR also insisted that its armistice agreements with Bulgaria, Finland, Hungary and Romania should form the basis of the subsequent peace treaties. To save the negotiations from a complete breakdown James Byrnes, the American Secretary of State (Foreign Minister), went to Moscow, where after some hard bargaining a compromise was reached whereby the Eastern European and the Italian peace treaties would be negotiated simultaneously. Negotiations dragged on for over a year and were frequently threatened by the escalating tension between the USSR and the Western Powers. Nevertheless in the final analysis both sides wanted the peace treaties concluded and were able to make compromises. As a concession to the USSR, the Treaty with Italy was harsh – it lost both Trieste, which became a self-governing 'Free Territory', and its colonies as well as having to pay reparations. In Eastern Europe the USSR gained what it wanted, particularly in the question of keeping troops in Romania to guard its lines of communication with Austria. The Peace Treaties with Italy and the minor Axis states were signed on 10 February 1947, but disagreements about the value of former German property to be handed over to the USSR delayed the Austrian treaty until 1955, while no treaty could be signed with Germany until an independent central German government had been restored.

3 | Germany, June 1945–April 1947

> **KEY ISSUE** Why did the four occupying Powers fail to work out a joint programme for Germany's future?

Germany's position in the middle of Europe and its potential wealth and military and economic strength ensured that neither the USSR nor the Western Allies could allow the other to dominate it. Indeed, as tension rose, both sides began to wonder whether Germany itself could not perhaps be enlisted as a future ally in a possible East–West conflict.

Germany in 1945

a) The Initial Period of Great Power Control of Germany, June 1945–November 1946

In June 1945 Stalin told a group of German Communists that there would be 'two Germanies' and then nine months later he informed the Yugoslavs that 'all Germany must be ours'.[2] Yet for a time he seemed ready to cooperate with the Western Powers in creating a new democratic Germany, in which the Communist Party, as in France and Italy, would play an important though not dominating role. This may well have been the reason why in June 1945 the USSR was the first occupying Power to license democratic parties in its Zone. At first the USSR was also a more cooperative partner on the Control Council than France. In the Autumn of 1945 the Russians were ready to agree to setting up a central German transport ministry and a national federation of trade unions, but both these proposals were defeated by French opposition to restoring a united Germany, which might again dominate Europe.

Why then was this cooperation not maintained? In the first place there were many high ranking British and American officials, as well as West German politicians, like Konrad Adenauer, the future West German Chancellor, who were convinced that the Soviet Zone was lost to the rest of Germany. The historian Willy Loth has also argued that Stalin's approach was not fully grasped by his officials in the Soviet Zone, who tended naturally to rely on local German Communists and to see middle class Germans as the class enemy. As in Poland, the NKVD and the Soviet army did not hesitate to arrest anybody who got in their way, which inevitably created a climate of 'latent fear'.[3]

It was this atmosphere that made a voluntary amalgamation in the Soviet Zone of the revived German Social Democratic (SPD) and Communist (KPD) parties impossible to achieve without the use of force. After the poor showing of the Communist party in the Hungarian elections of November 1945, Stalin realised that only a union between the SPD and KPD could create a strong friendly party in Germany. In an effort to win over the SPD the Soviets did force the KPD to make considerable concessions, but the threats and violence used by the Soviet Military Administration effectively disguised their extent, and alienated many SPD members. In the end after 20,000 Social Democrats had been interrogated, imprisoned and in some cases even murdered, the Central Executive of the SPD in the Soviet Zone agreed to the formation of a new united party, the Socialist Unity Party (SED), by a vote of 8 to 3 in February 1946. The Russians were then embarrassed when a month later a referendum on the decision was held in Berlin for members of both parties. In East Berlin they managed to close down the polling stations, but in the West voting went ahead and 82 per cent of the SPD members opposed the union. Inevitably, as with the USSR's actions in Poland, this only served to confirm the West's suspicions of Soviet policy.

At the end of April 1946 Stalin took stock of the situation in Germany, and in an important directive to his officials in the Soviet Zone he announced:

1 from the standpoint of the Soviet Union, it is not yet time to establish central authorities nor in general to continue with a policy of central-ization in Germany. The first goal, organizing the Soviet occupation Zone under effective Soviet control, has been more or less achieved.
5 The moment has thus now come to reach into the Western Zones. The instrument is the United Socialist-Communist Party. Some time will have to elapse before the party is organised in an orderly fashion in Greater Berlin itself, and this process will take even longer in the Western Zones. Only when the Soviet vision has been realized and the
10 Unity Party has established itself in the Western Zones, will the time have come to address once again the question of central Administrations and of effective Soviet support for a policy of central-ization in Germany.

The reason why Stalin wanted to delay setting up a central adminis-tration in Germany was that he suspected that the Americans and British were aiming to end the occupation of Germany as soon as possible because of the heavy financial burden it imposed on them. If that happened, he feared that the guarantees agreed on at Potsdam would be abandonded and that an aggressive and capitalist Germany would re-emerge.

b) The Problem of Reparations and the Creation of Bizonia

By the Spring of 1946 the compromise over reparations, which had been negotiated in Potsdam was already breaking down. As the Western Zones, particularly the heavily populated British Zone, were taking the majority of the German refugees expelled by the Poles and Czechs, Britain and America were anxious to encourage a moderate German economic recovery so that their Zones could at least pay for their own food imports. Consequently until that point was reached, they wished to delay delivering to the USSR the quotas from their own zones of machinery and raw materials, which had been agreed upon at Potsdam (see page 36). There was even talk that the Soviet Zone would have to deliver food to the hard pressed Western zones. In May General Clay, the Military Governor of the American Zone, in an attempt to bring the French into line and to force the Soviets to treat Germany as an economic unity, announced that no further reparation deliveries would be made until there was an overall plan for the German economy. To the Soviets it seemed that the Americans were bringing pressure to bear on them to agree to a reconstructed German economy within an international capitalist system. In June they responded to this threat by increasing production in their Zone and transforming 213 German firms into special Soviet joint stock companies, the total production of which was to go straight to the USSR.

When the Conference of Foreign Ministers returned to the question of Germany in July, Molotov, the Soviet Foreign Minister, insisted that the Germans should pay the USSR the equivalent of 10 billion dollars in reparations. Byrnes again argued that reparations could only be paid once Germany had a trade surplus that would cover the cost of food and raw material imports. He then offered to unify the American Zone economically with the other three Zones (see map page 38). Only Britain, which was finding its Zone a major drain on its fragile economy accepted. In retrospect this was a major step in the division of Germany between East and West, although its significance was initially played down. When the British and American Zones were merged economically in January 1947 to form what became called Bizonia, the Americans argued that, far from breaking the Potsdam agreement, the amalgamation would serve as an economic magnet to attract the French and Soviet Zones and so create the economic preconditions for fulfilling the Potsdam Agreement. In an attempt to convince the USSR that Bizonia was not an embryonic state the offices responsible for food, finance and transport were deliberately located in different cities.

c) The Moscow Conference of Foreign Ministers March–April 1947

The Moscow Conference was one of the turning points in early postwar history. The Russians made a determined effort to destroy Bizonia by demanding that a new central German administration under four Power control should be immediately set up. They ran into strong opposition from the British Foreign Secretary, Ernest Bevin, who feared that this would slow up the economic recovery of the British Zone. In London his officials had skilfully drawn up a plan for revising the Potsdam Agreement, which Bevin knew the Soviets could not accept. The USSR would, for instance, have actually to return some of the reparations, which it had seized in its Zone to help balance the budgets in the Western Zones, and it would receive no coal or steel deliveries until the whole of Germany could pay for its own food and raw material imports. Bevin successfully managed to manoeuvre the USSR into a corner when he persuaded the Americans to agree that political unity could only come *after* economic unity. As this would mean a protracted delay in reparation deliveries, the Soviets had little option but to reject the proposal, which is exactly what the Western Powers hoped they would do.

To the British and Americans the Moscow Conference was a 'successful failure'[4] in that it enabled them to press on with building up

Bizonia. Nothing, however, was decided on the divisive issues of reparations, and the future of Germany was left to dominate the agenda of the next conference scheduled to meet in London in November (see page 56).

4 The Truman Doctrine of Containment

KEY ISSUES What events led to the formulation of the Truman doctrine and what were the main points of this doctrine?

In June 1945 the Americans had assumed that Britain would continue to play a major role in the Eastern Mediterranean, but by January 1947 Britain faced a crippling economic crisis. As a result of political unrest in India, Palestine and Egypt and the long delay in completing the postwar peace treaties, Britain had to keep a large number of troops in Germany, Italy, the Middle East and Asia. This was, of course, enormously expensive, and by January 1947 the postwar American loan of 3.75 billion pounds had nearly been used up. The situation was made worse by the heavy blizzards and exceptionally cold weather that had brought transport, industry and coal mining virtually to a halt for several weeks. On 21 February the British in desperation informed the Americans that their financial and military aid to both Greece and Turkey would have to cease on 31 March.

This was very unwelcome news to Washington, as civil war had broken out again in Greece in May 1946. Truman feared above all that the Communists might launch a similar uprising in Italy once Allied troops had left after the signature of the peace treaty. He felt therefore that he had to act quickly to strengthen non-Communist forces in areas which were vulnerable to Soviet pressure, but to do this he required money, which could only be found by persuading Congress (parliament) to vote the necessary funds. On 12 March in a deliberately dramatic speech designed to appeal to Congress he stressed the seriousness of the international situation and how Europe was increasingly becoming divided into two mutually hostile blocs:

1 One way of life is based upon the will of the majority, and is distinguished by free institutions, representative government, free elections, guarantees of individual liberty, freedom of speech and religion, and freedom from political oppression. The second way of life is based upon
5 the will of a minority forcibly imposed upon the majority. It relies upon terror and oppression, a controlled press and radio, fixed elections and the suppression of personal freedoms.

I believe that it must be the policy of the United States to support free peoples who are resisting attempted subjugation by armed minorities

10 or by outside pressures. I believe that we must assist free peoples to work out their own destinies in their own way .... The seeds of totalitarian regimes are nurtured by misery and want. They spread and grow in the evil soil of poverty and strife. They reach their full growth when the hope of a people for a better life has died.

Initially Stalin dismissed this speech as an exercise in propaganda, but it soon became clear that it marked a new and important American policy initiative, which was to lead to what became called the Marshall Plan.

5 The Marshall Plan and the Soviet Response

> **KEY ISSUES** What were the aims of the Marshall plan and why did the USSR reject it?

Since 1945 the Americans had been pumping money into Western Europe in an attempt to prevent famine and total economic collapse. Two years later influential American journalists and politicians were beginning to argue that only through political and economic integration could Western Europe solve the whole complex of problems facing it. This would create a large and potentially prosperous market, which would act as a barrier to the further spread of Communism, and perhaps in time even pull the Eastern European states out of the Soviet bloc. It would also build a political structure into which West Germany, or indeed the whole of Germany, could be integrated and so contained.

In June 1947 after extensive consultations in Washington General George Marshall, the new American Secretary of State, made his historic offer of an aid package for Europe. The key to it was that:

... there must some agreement among the countries of Europe as to the requirements of the situation and the part those countries themselves will take in order to give proper effect to whatever action might be undertaken by this Government.

Stalin suspected that the offer masked an attempt by the USA to interfere in the domestic affairs of the European states, but he sent Molotov to Paris to discuss further details with the British and French. The Soviets certainly wanted financial credits from the USA but without any conditions attached. Britain and France, however, argued that a joint European programme should be drawn up rather than each individual state sending in a separate list of requests. On Stalin's orders Molotov rejected this and left the Conference. Stalin feared that a joint programme would enable American economic power to undermine Soviet influence in Eastern Europe. Bevin, who had done much to engineer this break, as he did not want to run the risk of the

USSR obstructing talks with the Americans, observed that Molotov's departure marked the beginning of the formation of a Western bloc.

On 16 July detailed negotiations on the Marshall Plan began in Paris where 16 Western European nations, including Turkey and Greece, were represented. Relevant information on Bizonia was provided by the occupation authorities. The Eastern European states were invited but stopped by Stalin from attending. For the Western Powers this simplified the negotiations, but even so, agreement was difficult to arrive at. Each Western European state had its own agenda. The French, for instance, wanted to ensure that their own economy had preference over the economic needs of Bizonia. They were, however, ready to consider the formation of a customs union, as long as it enabled France to control the West German economy. The British on the other hand wished to safeguard their sovereignty and were opposed to creating powerful supranational (transcending national limits) organisations. By mid-August the Americans were disappointed to find that the West Europeans had not come up with any radical plans for economic integration, and had only produced a series of national 'shopping lists'. Jefferson Caffery, the American Ambassador in Paris, complained that this simply recreated prewar economic conditions with all the 'low labor productivity and maldistribution of effort which derive from segregating 270,000,000 people into 17 uneconomic principalities'.[5] The Western European states also asked for 29 billion dollars, far more than Congress was ready to grant. To avoid the conference ending in failure, Bevin called an emergency meeting in Paris, which decided to let the Americans themselves propose where cuts in this sum could be made. The American officials immediately set up an 'Advisory Steering Committee', which attempted to bring the Europeans into line with essential American requirements, but by late September Washington had achieved only a limited success:

- Although the 16 states promised to liberalise trade and France to start negotiations for a customs union, these commitments were hedged around with qualifications aimed at protecting national independence.
- Germany's economic revival was declared essential, although it was to be carefully controlled to protect its neighbours.
- There was to be cooperation on the development of hydro-electric sources, pooling of railway wagons and the setting up of production targets for coal, agriculture, refined oil and steel.
- But there were to be no supranational authorities that could force the individual states to carry out these policies. At most the 16 states promised to set up a joint organisation to review how much progress was being made.

Stalin's decision to put pressure on the Eastern European states to boycott the Paris Conference marked the end of his attempts to cooperate with the United States and maintain the Grand Alliance. In September he invited the leaders of the Eastern European, French and Italian Communist parties to a conference at Szklarska Poreba in Poland to discuss setting up the Communist Information Bureau (COMINFORM), which would coordinate the policies and tactics of the Communist Parties in both the satellite states and in Western Europe. Andrei Zhdanov, Stalin's representative, told the delegates that the world was now divided into two hostile camps: the imperialist bloc led by the USA, intent on 'the enslavement of Europe,' and the 'anti-imperialist and democratic camp' led by the USSR. From this it followed that the whole policy of cooperating with moderate Socialist and Liberal parties would have to be abandoned and, where possible, Communist parties would have to take over power themselves and create societies whose economy and social system would be modelled on the Soviet system. From now on, as Martin McCauley has put it, 'there was to be only one road to socialism ...'.[6]

6 The Division Widens: The European States, June 1945–December 1947

> **KEY ISSUE** How and why was Europe increasingly divided into two blocs between June 1945 and December 1947?

In his famous speech at Fulton in the USA on 5 March 1946 Churchill made the following observation:

1   From Stettin in the Baltic, to Trieste, in the Adriatic, an iron curtain has descended across the continent. Behind that line lie all the capitals of the ancient states of Central and Eastern Europe – Warsaw, Berlin, Prague, Vienna, Belgrade, Bucharest and Sofia. All these famous cities,
5   and the populations around them, lie in the Soviet sphere, and all are subject in one form or another, not only to Soviet influence, but to a very high and increasing measure of control from Moscow. Athens alone ... is free to decide its future ....

How accurate was this analysis? Up to the Spring of 1947 it can be argued that 'diversity rather than uniformity'[7] still characterised the situation in Europe. Yugoslavia and Albania had their own Communist regimes, whose aggressive plans for a Balkan union and meddling in Greek domestic affairs Stalin at first attempted to control. Poland and Romania, both vital to the USSR's security, underwent Socialist revolutions and were in effect already Soviet satellites. In Hungary, Czechoslovakia, Finland and even Bulgaria Stalin pursued a more moderate policy of influence rather than direct control. With the escalation of the Cold War brought about by the Marshall Plan discussions and the creation of the COMINFORM, Stalin began to impose a much more uniform pattern on Eastern Europe. In Western Europe the intensifying Cold War polarised domestic politics. Communist parties were forced out of coalitions in France and Italy. Only in Finland did the situation remained unchanged.

a) Poland

To deflect Western criticism from his Polish policy Stalin had set up a provisional Government of National Unity in June 1945, which had been joined by Stanislaw Mikolajczyk, the former leader of the Government in exile in London. Stalin could not risk genuinely free elections as the Communist Party would inevitably suffer defeat. Mikolajczyk therefore resigned in protest from the provisional Cabinet in August 1945, and in October 1946 he refused to allow his party, the Polish Peasants' Party, to join the Communist dominated electoral bloc, which would present the electors with a single list of candidates. He hoped that this boycott would trigger a political crisis that would force Britain and the USA to intervene. In fact the new doctrine of containment being worked out by Truman accepted unofficially that Poland was within the USSR's sphere of interest and that the USA would not intervene in its domestic affairs. Thus when Mikolajczyk suggested that Britain and America should send officials to monitor the election in January 1947, both declined in the knowledge that there was little they could do to influence events in Poland. The results were a foregone conclusion. The Bloc, which used terror and falsified results with impunity, officially gained 394 seats, while the Peasants' Party gained a mere 28.

Although Gomulka, the leader of the Polish Communist Party, was dependent on Soviet assistance, he believed passionately that Poland had a unique history and could not just follow unquestioningly the Soviet example. He therefore viewed with dismay the creation of the Cominform, as he feared that it would force the Eastern European Communist parties to follow down to the last detail the Moscow model of Socialism. Only under considerable pressure did he reluctantly accept it, and a year later Stalin had him removed from the leadership (see page 58).

b) Romania and Bulgaria

The Soviet Union's claim that Romania was a vital security zone continued to meet with considerable understanding from the Western Powers. There was no strong opposition leader there like Mikolajczyk, and consequently the Soviets were able to consolidate their position more quickly than they did in Poland. In March 1946 the Socialist Party agreed to amalgamate with the Communists and in November the voters were presented with an electoral bloc, which even the opposition joined. Not surprisingly it won 80 per cent of the vote.

Soviet techniques and policy were similar in Bulgaria, although Stalin hoped to avoid unnecessary friction with the Western Powers until the peace treaty had been signed. In December 1945 he therefore forced the Communist dominated Bulgarian Government to include two members of the opposition, but when these began to demand changes in policy, Stalin advised the Communists to 'take a series of thought-out and well organized measures to smother the opposition'. Yet with an eye on the still unfinished peace treaties he remained anxious to mask the party's dictatorship. He even urged the sceptical Bulgarian Communists in September 1946 to set up a 'Labour Party', which would have 'a broader base and a better mask for the present period'.[8]

In October elections took place for a national assembly. The opposition parties managed to win over a third of the total votes, but Western hopes that this would form the basis of an effective parliamentary opposition were soon dashed. The Truman Doctrine and increasing American involvement in Greece meant that Bulgaria became a front line state in the defence of Communism. Consequently Stalin allowed the Communists to liquidate the opposition. The Bulgarian Communist Party also took the creation of the Cominform as a cue for pressing on with its radical programme for nationalising industry, collectivising agriculture and creating a one party state.

c) Yugoslavia

Yugoslavia occupied a unique position amongst the Soviet dominated states in Eastern and South Eastern Europe, as the Communist Party had effectively won power independently of the Soviet forces. The People's Front dominated by the Yugoslav Communist party won 90 per cent of the votes in the election of November 1945, and Tito was then able smoothly to implement a revolution based on the Stalinist model in the USSR. Tito had his own plans for making Yugoslavia the major regional power in South East Europe. Only the continued presence of British and American troops stopped him from annexing Trieste in the period 1945–48, when he was perceived by the West, not entirely accurately, to be acting as the proxy of the USSR. Yet his dramatic break with Stalin in 1948 was to change this assessment (see page 59).

d) Hungary and Czechoslovakia

Up to the Autumn of 1947 Stalin appeared to be interested primarily in preserving a strong Communist influence in Czechoslovakia and Hungary rather than in complete domination. In Czechoslovakia the postwar social revolution had been carried out by an alliance of Socialists and Communists under the direction of President Benes. Soviet troops had been withdrawn as early as December 1945. The elections in May 1946, in which the Communists won some 38 per cent of the vote, were carried out without any violence or efforts by the Communist Party to manipulate the vote. Although Gottwald had established a tight grip on the Czech security forces, he had no plans for a coup and appeared to pin his hope on winning the 1948 election. Without the intensifying Cold War Czechoslovakia might perhaps have remained a bridge between East and West, as Benes had hoped, but the Marshall Plan and the subsequent creation of COMINFORM effectively created a climate where this was impossible. The Czech Cabinet vetoed this and voted unanimously in July to attend the Paris Conference on the Plan, but the Soviet government insisted that the Americans under cover of offering a loan were 'trying to form a Western bloc and isolate the Soviet Union'. Czech proposals for compromise were ruthlessly dismissed. Jan Masaryk, the Foreign Minister, later told the British Ambassador: 'I went to Moscow as the Foreign Minister of an independent sovereign state; I returned as a lackey of the Soviet Government'.[9] What this implied became clearer at Szklarska Poreba in September when the Secretary-General of the Czech Communist Party, Rudolf Slansky, told the conference that the reactionary forces would have to be expelled from the National Front.

It seemed in the Autumn of 1945 that Hungary, like Czechoslovakia, was treated as a special case by Stalin. The elections of November 1945 were free, even though the Soviets could have influenced them easily. Two years later the press was still free as was debate in parliament, the borders with the West were open and most small and medium sized business were in private hands. Yet until the signing of the Peace Treaty Soviet influence was guaranteed through its dominating position on the ACC, and Stalin was able to insist on the Communist party participating in the Coalition Government and controlling the vital Ministry of the Interior. In the Spring of 1947 the most powerful opposition to the Communists was shattered, when the leader of the Smallholders party, Bela Kovacs, was arrested by Russian troops for conspiring against the occupation. Yet even this did not lead to an overwhelming Communist success in the August elections when the Left bloc only won 45 per cent of the vote. As late as the Autumn of 1947, it still seemed possible that Hungary might retain some independence, but it was increasingly being drawn into the Soviet bloc. On 8 December a Treaty of Friendship and cooperation was signed with Yugoslavia and, a month later, a mutual aid treaty with the USSR.

e) France and Italy

Initially after liberation the French Government attempted to balance between the USSR and the Western Powers. Indeed many historians argue that France did not really join the Cold War on the side of

Britain and America until the Moscow Conference of March 1947. However, the French historian, Annie Lacroix Riz, has shown that long before then Paris had unofficially aligned itself with Britain and the USA. As early as October 1945 General de Gaulle was thinking of a Western European Defence Organisation with an American and possibly even a German contribution, but when he fell from power, the new government, a Communist, Socialist and Christian Democrat coalition, attempted to act as a bridge between East and West. Even then, though, to quote Georges-Henri Soutou, 'behind the scenes and in the utmost secrecy'[10] the Christian Democrats and some of the Socialists attempted to draw nearer to America. In March 1946 the French Socialist leader, Leon Blum, went to Washington to negotiate an American loan, and quite voluntarily accepted the American arguments for free international trade, which effectively meant France's inclusion in the capitalist Western world. At the Moscow Conference in March 1947 France openly aligned itself with the British and Americans, and two months later the Communist were expelled from the governing coalition. Initially they remained allied with the Socialists, but in the autumn Stalin ordered them to stage a series of violent strikes against the Marshall Plan. This finally persuaded the Socialists to distance themselves from them and to accept the pro-American policy of the Christian Democrats.

There was a similar pattern of events in Italy. The Communists joined the coalition government in April 1945, and some Italian statesmen argued that Italy should try to balance between the USSR and the Western Powers. Yet essentially Italy, as Stalin himself conceded, had little option but to support the latter group, since it had been liberated and occupied by them. In December 1945 a new coalition government was created under de Gasperi, a Christian Democrat, who rapidly won American support for his economic policies. As East–West tension grew in 1946–47, the Italian Government moved to the Right, and in May 1947 the Communists were dismissed from the cabinet. This cleared the way for the Government to accept the Marshall Plan and to align itself unambiguously with the West.

f) Finland

Finland again remained the exception to the pattern developing in the other European states. Its weak Communist Party received little help from the USSR. Why was this so? Ulam argues that Finland escaped being integrated into the Soviet bloc merely by chance, as Zhdanov, the Soviet chairman of the ACC, was away most of the time in Moscow working in the Central Committee of the Communist party. Yet Jukka Nevakivi, who has studied the relevant Soviet sources, argues that Stalin simply wanted to neutralise Finland, and once the Finns had signed the Treaty of friendship, Cooperation and Mutual Assistance in 1948, he was ready to leave them alone.[11]

7 Assessment

> **KEY ISSUE** Was the break up of the Grand Alliance in the period
> 1945–47 more a result of Soviet or American policies?

How inevitable was the break up of the Grand Alliance by the
Autumn of 1947? We have seen its real glue was Hitler. Once Nazi
Germany and Imperial Japan were defeated, it was always more likely
that it would disintegrate than remain intact. Stalin was quite determined to turn Poland, Romania and Bulgaria into satellite states
regardless of what the liberal West might think about the violation of
democracy or human rights. On the other hand, he did have a 'differentiated' policy, which for two years allowed Hungary and
Czechoslovakia to be 'bridges' to the West. Is it an exaggeration
therefore to say that Stalin pursued a relatively moderate line in
Eastern Europe up to 1947, and that his German policy, rather than
a result of deep laid plans to take over the former Reich, was more a
clumsy attempt to neutralise it, and gain the vital reparations needed
by the USSR? Michael Mccgwire has argued that Stalin was actively
seeking to preserve the 'remaining shreds of the collaborative
wartime relationship',[12] and as a consequence of this had by 1947
lost his chance to control Greece and allow Yugoslavia to seize
Trieste. By the Spring and Summer of 1947 Stalin was thrown on the
defensive first by the Truman Doctrine and then by the Marshall
Plan.

Does this mean that Truman in fact started the Cold War? The
Truman Doctrine and the Marshall Plan were certainly important
thresholds in the Cold War, but the context in which the Americans
acted is also important. The seismic events of early 1947 – Britain's
near bankruptcy and withdrawal from the Eastern Mediterranean,
growing economic paralysis in Germany and the strength of the
Communist parties in Italy and France – galvanised the Americans
into announcing first the Truman Doctrine and then the Marshall
Plan. This was the turning point in the immediate postwar period and
provoked the USSR into tightening its grip on Eastern Europe and
creating the Cominform.

References

1 M. Smith, *Emperor's Circle* (Bantam, 2000).
2 J. Gaddis, *We Now Know* (OUP, 1997), p. 116.
3 W. Loth, *Stalin's Unwanted Child: The German Question and the Founding of
the GDR* (Macmillan, 1998), p. 25.
4 *Ibid.*, p. 62.
5 M.J. Hogan, 'The Marshall Plan' in C.S. Maier (ed.), *The Cold War in
Europe*, 3rd edn (Markus Wiener, Princeton, 1996), p. 219.
6 M. McCauley, *The Origins of the Cold War* (Longman, 1983), p. 74.

7 G. Swain and N. Swain, *Eastern Europe since 1945*, 2nd edn (St. Martin's Press, 1998), p. 48.

8 Quotations from V. Dimitrov, 'Revolution Released: Stalin, the Bulgarian Communist Party and the Establishment of the Cominform' in F. Gori and S. Pons (eds.), *The Soviet Union and Europe in the Cold War, 1943–53* (St. Martin's Press, 1996), pp. 282 & 284.

9 Quotations from I. Lukes, 'The Czech Road to Communism' in N. Naimark and L. Gibianskii, *The Establishment of Communist Regimes in Eastern Europe, 1944–49* (Boulder, Colorado, 1997), p. 250.

10 G.-H. Soutou, 'France' in D. Reynolds (ed.), *The Origins of the Cold War in Europe* (Yale UP, 1994), p. 101.

11 See J. Nevakivi, 'The Soviet Union and Finland after the War, 1944–53' in Gori and Pons, *op.cit.*, pp. 89–103.

12 M. Mcgwire, 'National Security and Soviet Foreign Policy' in M. Leffler and S. Painter, *Origins of the Cold War* (Routledge, 1994), p. 55.

Summary Diagram
The Break up of the Grand Alliance, 1945–7

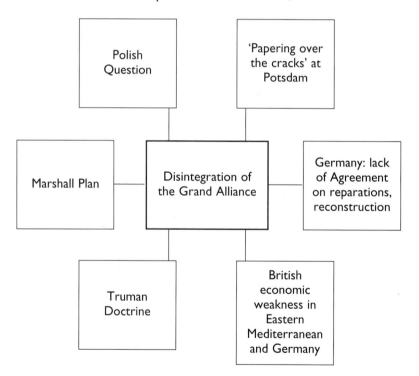

Working on Chapter 3

In making notes you should concentrate on identifying the key factors that led to the breakdown of the alliance and then show why they did so. You should therefore consider whether Potsdam was an ambiguous and inadequate settlement and why the occupying Powers could not agree on the future of Germany. Look carefully, too, at the consequences of the Truman Doctrine and the Marshall Plan. Finally consider the impact of these events on the individual European states and ask yourself to what extent was Churchill right that an 'iron curtain' divided Europe?

Answering structured and essay questions on Chapter 3

This chapter has involved a fairly detailed examination of why the Grand Alliance broke up. It is important to have a good knowledge of this complex period, as it explains much of the origins of the Cold War. Look at the following structured questions:

1. **a)** Why was the SED formed in 1946 and why did it alarm the Western Powers and the Western Germans?
    b) What was Bizonia and why was its creation opposed by the USSR?
    c) Explain why reparations were such a divisive issue in Germany.
2. **a)** What was the Truman Doctrine and why was it formulated?
    b) What did the Americans hope that the Marshall Plan would achieve?
    c) Why did the USSR oppose the Marshall Plan?

These questions are testing both your factual knowledge and understanding of the period. In 1a) and b) explaining why the Soviets formed the SED and what Bizonia was is fairly straightforward, but the second part of both questions as well as 1c) require more analytical explanations from you. To show why the SED alarmed the Western Powers and the creation of Bizonia, the USSR, you will need to consider what the real and perceived motives behind these actions were. In 2a) the first part of the question requires a relatively simple explanation, but the follow-up question again requires rather more thought from you. To what extent did Truman exaggerate the Soviet threat to impress Congress? Questions 2b) also needs rather more that a simple factual answer. Were the Americans generously coming to the rescue of the Europeans or were they hoping to build up a market in Europe for American exports? Perhaps it was a mixture of both factors? Question 2c) is really a follow-on from b). Having explained in b) the motives behind the Marshall Plan and how the Americans hoped it would work, it is possible to explain why the USSR feared that the Plan would loosen its grip on Eastern Europe.

In essay questions you will be confronted with much more wide-ranging questions, which require a detailed knowledge of events from the end of the war up to the autumn of 1947. The basic question on the beginning of the Cold War is 'Why did the Grand Alliance fall apart so quickly'? Most other essay questions on this period are variations of the same theme. Consider these examples:

1. Was disagreement on Germany the cause of the break up of the Grand Alliance?
2. 'It was the USA rather than the USSR which was responsible for the break up of the Grand Alliance'. Discuss.
3. To what extent was the Marshall Plan the trigger for the Cold War?

All three of these questions require a detailed knowledge of the years 1945–47. They each put forward a different but important reason for the break up of the Grand Alliance: disagreement on Germany, the USA or the Marshall Plan. You must, of course, consider these points carefully as they are all major contributions to the causes of the Cold War, but you must also point out that they are only part of the story. Disagreement on Germany was certainly a major factor, but it also needs to be seen in the context of Soviet policy in Poland, the 'Iron Curtain', the vulnerability of Western Europe and the collapse of British power. Question 2 is deliberately provocative and invites you to consider the revisionist case against the USA, but here again you must not negelect to analyse the impact on the West of Soviet policy in Germany and Eastern Europe. Question 3 requires an analysis of the Marshall Plan and the Soviet response, but you will also need to ask yourself why the USA formulated it. Was it a response to perceived Soviet threats or an example of American 'economic imperialism'?

Source-based questions on Chapter 3

1 Stalin, Truman and the Causes of the Cold War
Look at the cartoon on page 35 and read the extracts from Churchill's speech at Fulton on page 45, Stalin's directive of April 1946 on page 40 and Truman's speech before the American Congress on 12 March 1947 on pages 42–3, and then answer the following questions:

a) Assess the value of the cartoon to an historian studying the role of America in early postwar Europe. (*6 marks*)
b) Study the extract on page 40.
   i) Why does Stalin think that it is not yet time to set up a central government in Germany? (*3 marks*)
   ii) What does Stalin mean by his statement that the 'moment has thus come to reach into the Western Zones' (line 5)? (*4 marks*)

c) Study the extract on pages 42–3.
  i) What does Truman mean by the 'seeds of totalitarian regimes are nurtured by misery and want' (lines 11–12)? (*3 marks*)
  ii) How does Truman differentiate between the two 'ways of life' he describes? (*4 marks*)
d) Study the extracts on pages 40 and 42–3.
  How valid is Stalin's directive for helping one understand the background to Truman's speech to Congress on 12 March 1947? (*5 marks*)
e) Using these extracts and your own knowledge of the period assess how accurate Churchill was in his analysis of the situation developing in Europe in the Spring of 1946 (page 45). (*10 marks*)

Source questions often contain cartoons. Through exaggeration the cartoonist sets out to make a powerful comment on current events. Always ask yourself what is the message that the cartoon is communicating about the events or people portrayed. Here President Truman, dressed up as the Statute of Liberty, is holding the keys to both financial and military power, which America's wartime allies are desperate to get their hand on. Is this a perceptive comment on the situation in December 1945?

Usually at least one source question asks you to use 'your own knowledge' or 'any other evidence known to you', while also looking, of course, at the given extracts. Questions like this are really mini-essays linked to specific sources. You must therefore take care to evaluate both the given extract, *and* draw on your own historical knowledge to add to it. Remember that 'assess' means that you must reach a judgement on whether the information at your disposal confirms the accuracy of the source you are asked to evaluate. Usually your sources will be contradictory, or one-sided, allowing you to reach only a qualified answer. Here for instance, Churchill was proved right in the medium term, but perhaps he exaggerated the situation in March 1946?

4 The Division of Germany and Europe, 1948–9

POINTS TO CONSIDER

This chapter covers the crucial two years from the collapse of the London Conference in December 1947 to the creation of the German Democratic Republic in October 1949. It is the period when not only Germany but Europe was divided into two blocs dominated by the USA and USSR. As you read this chapter, ask yourself not only how the blocs differed from each other, but whether the division of Europe could have been avoided. Was it caused by the USA's attempt to encourage European economic integration based on the American model and the decision by the Western Allies to go ahead with building up a separate West German state as an effective barrier against Communism? Was the Berlin blockade in reality just a clumsy defensive reaction by the USSR to threatening Western initiatives? On the other hand, you may come to the conclusion that Stalin's foreign policy represented a real threat to the West, which more than justified its independent action in West Germany, the signature of the Brussels Pact and the creation of NATO.

KEY DATES

1947	15 Dec	Break up of London Foreign Ministers' Conference.
1948	22 Feb	Communist coup in Czechoslovakia.
	17 March	Brussels Pact signed.
	7 June	London 6-Power Conference recommends calling of a West German Constituent Assembly.
	20 June	Currency reform in Western zones.
	24 June	Berlin Blockade begins.
	5 Sept	Parliamentary Council meets in Bonn.
1949	4 Apr	NATO set up.
	12 May	USSR lifts Berlin Blockade.
	23 May	Basic law approved in FRG.
	30 May	Peoples' Congress approves GDR Constitution.
	22 Sept	Occupation Statute in force in FRG.
	12 Oct	GDR set up.

1 A Western Bloc Begins to Emerge

> **KEY ISSUES** Why did the Western European and North Atlantic states begin to form a Western bloc? What progress had been made by the autumn of 1949?

a) The London Conference of Foreign Ministers, November–December 1947

By the time the Conference opened in London the chances of any agreement on Germany seemed remote. The Americans vigorously supported the idea of Western European integration and had at least temporarily resigned themselves to the division of Germany. The USSR still wished to avoid the partition of Germany, as this would result in the great industrial complex of the Ruhr becoming a part of an American dominated Western European bloc, but its attempts to disrupt the Marshall Plan by orchestrating widespread strikes in Italy and France merely fuelled the mistrust of the Western Powers of Soviet intentions in Germany and indeed throughout Europe. The Soviets had also tried hard to rally public opinion right across Germany against the policy of the Western Allies. Walther Ulbricht, the leader of the SED, was instructed to organise a 'German People's Congress for Unity and a Just Peace'. Representatives from all parties throughout Germany were invited to attend its meetings on 6–7 December 1947 in Berlin. The intention was then to send a delegation to the London Conference to back up the Soviet demand for the formation of a German central government. Roughly one third of the 2,225 delegates came from the West, but these were overwhelmingly Communists from areas like the Ruhr and the big industrial towns. The movement did not therefore genuinely reflect West German opinion and Bevin refused to allow its delegation permission to enter Britain.

The London Conference broke up on 15 December 1947 amidst bitter recriminations. The Soviets accused Britain and America of violating the Potsdam Agreement and of denying the USSR its fair share of reparations, while the Western Powers rejected Soviet proposals for forming a central German government as they feared that it would only fall under Soviet control. All hope of four Power cooperation now disappeared, and instead the alternatives of a Western alliance, closer economic cooperation in Western Europe and the creation of a West German state appeared to be the only practical options. All three policies were interrelated and depended ultimately on the military and political integration of West Germany into a Western European defence system linked to the USA and directed against the USSR.

b) The Brussels Pact and 'Western Union'

However, the revival of even a weakened West Germany was still viewed with deep mistrust and fear by the French. In an effort to calm their anxieties the British came up with a plan for the formation of what they called with some exaggeration a 'Western Union'. Theoretically this was a defensive alliance against Germany, but in reality, as Paul-Henri Spaak, the Belgian prime minister, pointed out, it 'was meant as a screen behind which to consider defences against Russia',[1] as occupied Germany was hardly in a position to threaten its neighbours. The Communist seizure of power in Prague on 22 February (see page 58), was a powerful factor in persuading the French to join an alliance system directed primarily against the USSR rather than Germany. The French Government was also reassured by the American decision to keep troops in West Germany for the fore-seeable future.

On 17 March the Brussels Pact was signed by Belgium, Britain, France, Luxemburg and the Netherlands. It did not mention the USSR by name but simply promised mutual defence against an aggressor from any quarter. The treaty contained clauses on cultural and social cooperation and provision for setting up a 'Consultative Council'. This reflected Bevin's wish to encourage general Western European cooperation as a further barrier to the spread of Communism. Bevin intended that the Brussels Pact should be under-pinned by an Atlantic alliance in which the USA would be a key member. The Americans responded rapidly to this suggestion, and by the end of March the first of a series of secret meetings between British, Canadian and American officials began to explore the possi-bility of such an alliance. Eventually this was to lead to the signing of the North Atlantic Treaty (see page 64).

c) The Distribution of Marshall Aid and the Question of European Integration

The Americans intended, as Michael Hogan has said, to 'refashion' Western Europe 'in the image of the US'.[2] They were convinced that once an economically integrated and politically united Western Europe existed, it would rapidly become as wealthy as the United States. It would then simultaneously deter the USSR, significantly boost world trade and provide valuable markets for American exports. In the Spring of 1948 the American Congress approved a programme for $5 billion dollars as the first instalment of Marshall Aid. Washington then attempted to persuade the Western European states to set up an international committee, which would be power-ful enough to supervise the distribution of Marshall aid and enforce the integration of their economies. In response to this, the Organisation for European Economic Cooperation (OEEC) was set up, but each state still had its own national agenda, especially Britain, which was determined not to surrender any power to a supranational organisation. Effectively this defeated American attempts to use Marshall Aid as a means to create an integrated Western Europe in the American image, although over the next three years the Europeans themselves were to develop their own path to integration.

2 The Consolidation of the Eastern Bloc

> **KEY ISSUE** How did Stalin strengthen Communism in the
> Eastern Bloc, 1947–48?

By June 1948 the Cominform (see page 45) had become a power-ful instrument for controlling the Soviet bloc. Theoretically each state in the bloc remained independent, but all had to adopt iden-tical cultural, military, economic and social policies. This meant an end to the policy of diversity that had characterized Eastern Europe for the first two years after the war. In Czechslovakia the Communists seized power at the end of February, while in Hungary they steadily strengthened their position throughout 1948. A Communist-dominated People's Independence Front was set up there, and in the elections in May 1949 only candidates approved by the Front could stand. In Poland Gomulka, who wished to create a Socialist society that would reflect the actual conditions in Poland rather than the USSR, was forced to resign in August 1948 and then imprisoned.

A NOTE ON THE COMMUNIST SEIZURE OF POWER IN CZECHOSLOVAKIA

The Prague coup did not come as a surprise to the Western Allies. In practice London, Washington and Paris had already written off Czechoslovakia and were not ready to intervene to save it from Communism. The Czech Communists, with nothing to fear from the West, were anxious to seize power as quickly as possible because their popularity was sharply declining and they were likely to suffer a severe defeat in the coming elections. The crisis point was reached on 13 February 1948 when the cabinet protested against the unfair demotion of eight senior non-Communist police officers. A week later in protest against the Communist Minister of Interior's refusal to intervene, 12 minis-ters resigned from the cabinet, hoping to bring down the Government, but this did not happen, as the Social Democrats and the two non-Party ministers, Masaryk and Svoboda, remained. The Communists were therefore able to use their con-trol of the trade unions and the police to seize power and force Benes to appoint a new cabinet, which would follow loyally the policies laid down in Moscow. The elections of 30 May were held on the basis of a single National Front list which committed all candidates to a manifesto approved by Moscow.

3 The Yugoslav–Soviet Split

> **KEY ISSUE** What caused the Yugoslav–Soviet split?

By the summer of 1948 Europe was not only divided into two blocs, but within the Soviet bloc there ran a split between the USSR and Yugoslavia that was every bit as deep and bitter. Although Tito had been publicly praised at the COMINFORM meeting in September 1947 as one of Stalin's most loyal and effective allies, Stalin nevertheless had some reservations about him. He was critical of Yugoslav attempts to play an independent role in the Balkans and of 'certain tendencies' among Yugoslav party leaders 'to overestimate their achievements'.[3]

In the course of the winter 1947/8 the friction between Moscow and Belgrade increased. Tito alarmed Stalin with talk about forming a South-Eastern European federation which would include Greece and Bulgaria. He was also planning to set up a military base in Albania. Stalin feared not only that this would make the Yugoslav Communist Party the strongest force in the Balkans, but that it would also provoke the USA at a time of escalating tension over Germany. Party delegations from Bulgaria and Yugoslavia were therefore summoned to Mocow and made to confess their 'mistakes'. Stalin specifically vetoed the stationing of Yugoslav troops in Albania, and, instead of the wider federation favoured by Tito, proposed a smaller Bulgarian–Yugoslav union. The two states also had to commit themselves from now on to regular consultations with Soviet officials on foreign policy questions. Tito refused to subordinate his foreign policy to Moscow, and rejected union with Bulgaria, as he feared that, given Soviet influence there, it would merely be a way for Stalin to tighten his grip on Yugoslavia. Stalin reacted to this open defiance of his leadership by turning the conflict into 'a head-on collision'.[4] He withdrew his advisers from Yugoslavia and accused its leaders of a long list of political and ideological 'crimes'. He also put pressure on the other East bloc states to support the Soviet line. By the time of the second COMINFORM meeting in June 1948 the whole Soviet bloc, as well as the West European Communist leaders, were united against Tito, who was then formally expelled from the organisation. Although many privately doubted the truth of Stalin's accusations, they supported them because in the final analysis, at a time of acute tension with the West triggered by the Berlin blockade, they were dependent on Moscow for their own survival. Only in Yugoslavia did a Communist Party have a base genuinely independent of the USSR.

4 The Decision to Create a West German State

> **KEY ISSUE** How was French opposition to setting up West Germany overcome at the London Conference (February–June 1948)?

The collapse of the London Foreign Ministers' Conference in December 1947 and the emergence of two rival power blocs in Europe strengthened the Western Allies in their resolve to form a separate West German state. How this was to be done was then discussed by Britain, France, the USA and the Benelux states at another conference in London, which sat, except for a break of six weeks in the middle, from 23 February to 2 June 1948.

Anglo-American Plans for creating a West German state were met with considerable hostility from France, which dreaded the revival of German power. Neither the British nor the Americans were ready to compromise on this, but as the new West German state was to be subjected to tight controls and the Americans had already committed themselves to joining a North Atlantic Treaty Alliance, French fears were to a certain extent appeased (see page 57). The production of the great industrial centre of the Ruhr was to be regulated by the International Ruhr Authority, which would be controlled by the Western Allies. The West Germans would also have to accept an occupation statute, which would give Britain, France and the USA far reaching powers over trade, foreign relations, economic questions and disarmament.

The West Germans were authorised on 7 June to draft a constitution for a democratic, federal West German state. On 20 June the Western Allies introduced the new currency, the *Deutschmark*, into the Western zones and four days later the Soviets responded by introducing the new East Mark into the their own Zone. With the introduction of the currency reforms the outline of the two German states was beginning to take shape.

5 The Soviet Response: The Berlin Blockade

> **KEY ISSUES** Why did the Soviets blockade West Berlin and why did this action fail?

a) Pressure on Berlin Begins

The Six Power London Conference and the Brussels Treaty had confronted the Soviets with a major challenge. Stalin, however, believed that he could force the Western Allies to reconsider the whole German question by applying pressure to their position in West Berlin, which was vulnerable as it was dependent on rail and road links running through the Soviet Zone for bulk supplies from the West. Consequently in March 1948 the Soviet occupying forces began to exercise an ever tighter control over the movement of people and freight from West Berlin to the Western Zones. The introduction of the *Deutschmark* first into the Western Zones and then into West Berlin on 23 June provided the Soviets with the necessary excuse to begin the full blockade of West Berlin. They argued that it was a defensive measure to stop the Soviet Zone being swamped with the

devalued *Reichsmarks*, which the new *Deutschmark* was replacing in West Germany. In the night of 23–24 June the blockade began. The rail and road links to the West as well as the supply of electricity from East Berlin to the Western sectors were all cut.

b) The Berlin Blockade, 24 June, 1948–12 May, 1949

The Western response was confused and unsure. The French were convinced that West Berlin could only hold out for a matter of weeks, while the American administration 'seemed almost paralysed by uncertainty and fear'.[5] It was Bevin who again provided the initial leadership of the alliance, and suggested forceful counter-measures. Essentially he was determined to maintain the Western position in Berlin and press on with setting up a West German state, while at all costs avoiding war. He rejected suggestions by General Clay, the American Military Governor, that an armed convoy should force its way through to West Berlin, because this could easily have provoked an armed clash with Soviet forces. Instead he convinced the Americans that West Berlin could be supplied by aircraft flying along the three 'corridors', or flight paths, allocated to the Western Allies by the Soviets in 1945 (see diagram, page 63). He also responded enthusiastically to American requests to transfer 60 B-29 bombers to East Anglia. It was assumed at the time that these carried atomic bombs, but in fact this was a bluff, as the modified B-29's, which could carry them, only arrived in Britain in 1949. Nevertheless this gesture probably did deter the Soviets from trying to interfere with the airlift, although they too wanted to avoid war. By the end of July British and American planes were managing to fly into West Berlin an average of 2,000 tons of food and raw materials a day. Yet if stocks were to be built up for the coming winter, 5,000 tons would have to be flown in on a regular daily basis.

As it was very uncertain whether these totals could be maintained, the three Western Powers were ready to explore the possibility of reaching an agreement over Berlin. On 2 August their ambassadors met Stalin in Moscow. Interpreting their approach as a sign of weakness, he was uncompromising over his demands. According to the Soviet record of the meeting on 2 August

1   Comrade Stalin spoke of two factors – the special currency in Berlin and the decisions of the London Conference. He thought that it was those decisions which gave rise to the restrictive measures under discussion ... Comrade Stalin said that ... simultaneously with the rescind-
5   ing of the restrictions on transport applied by the Soviet Military Administration, the special currency [the Deutschmark] ... introduced by the three powers into Berlin should be withdrawn and replaced by the currency circulating in the Soviet Zone .... That was the first point. Secondly, assurance should be given that application of the London

10 Conference's decisions would be postponed until representatives of the four powers had met and negotiated on all the basic questions concerning Germany.

West Berlin children watch an American plane, loaded with food, come in to land in early August 1948.

The Western Powers would not reverse their decision to create a West German state, but they were ready to agree to the circulation of the East Mark in the whole of Berlin, subject to Four Power financial control. Yet, as further discussions between the Military Governors of the four zones in September showed, the Soviets wanted total control of the currency. If they were to abandon the blockade, at the very least, they intended, as one Soviet official observed,

1 to restore the economic unity of Berlin, to include all Berlin in the economic system of the Soviet Zone and also to restore unified administration of the city. That would have served as a basis for winning over the population of West Berlin, and would have created the precondi-
5 tions for completely ousting the Western powers from Berlin.

These talks broke down on 7 September because neither side would give way. As the Soviets were convinced that the airlift to West Berlin could not be sustained during the winter, they decided to play for time and avoid any compromise. Consequently all the efforts of the United Nations during the winter of 1948/49 to mediate failed.

By the end of January 1949, however, it became clear that Stalin's gamble was also failing. The winter of 1948/9 was exceptionally mild, and, thanks to the effective deployment of the large American C54s, which flew to Berlin from bases in the British Zone, the average daily tonnage for January was 5,620. By April this had reached 8,000 tons per day and about 1000 aircraft were able to use the air corridors to Berlin at any one time (see diagram on page 63). In February the Western Powers also declared the *Deutschmark* to be the sole legal currency in West Berlin. Stalin, who was not prepared to go to war over Berlin, had little option but to cut his losses. In an interview with an American journalist on 31 January he made a considerable concession, when he indicated that he would make the lifting of the blockade dependent only on calling another meeting of the Council of Foreign Ministers. The Americans responded to this and talks began between the Soviet and US representatives in the Security Council. In early May they finally reached agreement that the blockade would be called off on 12 May and that eleven days later a Council of Foreign Ministers should meet in Paris to discuss both the future of Germany

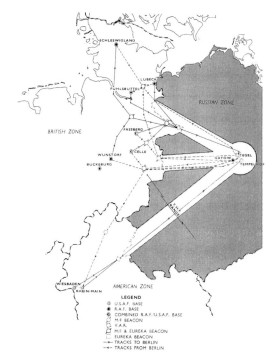

A diagram showing how the airlift worked. Radar beacons regulated the flow of aircraft before they entered the corridors to Berlin.

and the Berlin currency question. On neither issue did the Council produce a breakthrough, but the four Powers approved the New York agreement on lifting the blockade and agreed to talks on normalising as far as possible the life of the city.

6 The North Atlantic Treaty

> **KEY ISSUES** Why was the Treaty signed and to what extent was it a compromise between European and American wishes?

The Prague coup and the Berlin blockade finally persuaded the Americans that there was no alternative to a formal commitment to defend Western Europe. From the Spring of 1948 through to early 1949 the American government gradually worked out the framework for a North Atlantic–Western European military alliance with both Congressional leaders at home and its allies in Europe. Over the course of these negotiations it became increasingly clear that the proposed North Atlantic Treaty interlocked with the plans for setting up a West German state. Without this Treaty it would have been very difficult, perhaps even impossible, to have persuaded the French to tolerate the creation of West Germany, whose potential military and industrial power they still feared.

The American government had to take a middle line between the Europeans, who hoped for an alliance as closely defined as possible, and Congress, which wanted to avoid any precise commitments. To win over Congress Truman had to stress that the treaty did not commit the USA to go to war without its consent and that it would help the West Europeans to defend themselves. In the end the key Article 5 contained the rather imprecise wording that each treaty member 'will take such action as it deems necessary, including the use of armed force, to restore and maintain security in the North Atlantic area'. The West Europeans, particularly the French, found this too weak, but decided to use Article 3, which called for 'continuous and effective self help and mutual aid'[6] to involve the Americans ever more closely in the defence of Western Europe.

The North Atlantic Treaty (NATO) was signed on 4 April 1949 in Washington for an initial period of 20 years by Canada, the USA, the Brussels Pact Powers, Norway, Denmark, Iceland, Italy and Portugal, and it came into force on 24 August 1949. When the NATO Council met for the first time in September, Defence and Military Committees were set up and its members were divided into five regional groups to all of which the United States belonged. At the same time Congress approved a military assistance programme to help build up Western Europe's armed forces. These actions ended, for the time being anyway, the fears that the Europeans still had that the USA might again retire back into isolation as it had done in 1919.

7 The Division of Germany

> **KEY ISSUE** To what extent was East Germany set up in response to the creation of West Germany?

a) The Creation of the Federal Republic

The West German constitution was approved in the Spring of 1949 by the three Western occupying Powers, and elections for the new parliament (*Bundestag*) took place in August. A month later when parliament met, Konrad Adenauer became the first West German Chancellor. The Federal Republic (FRG) was, however, far from being independent. The Occupation Statute, which came into force in September, replaced the military government in the former Western zones with a High Commission. This still gave Britain, France and the USA the final say on West German foreign policy, security questions, exports and many other matters that an independent state is free to decide upon for itself.

b) The Emergence of the German Democratic Republic

In the winter of 1948–49 the Soviets were reluctant to set up a separate East German state if there was still a chance of stopping British and American plans for West Germany and of one day creating a neutral pro-Soviet Germany. Stalin was prepared to give the Soviet Zone greater administrative independence, but for the moment this was just a temporary step which would not block eventual German unity.

Throughout the Spring and Summer of 1949 Ulbricht and the other leaders of the Socialist Unity Party claimed that only their party was working for national unity in contrast to the 'splitters'[7] in the West. To emphasise this claim they set up in March 1948 a 'German People's Council' (*Volksrat*) of 400 delegates, a quarter of whom were Communists from the Western zones, to draft a constitution for a united German state. If a unified Germany proved impossible to create, then this constitution would form the basis of a new East German state. In May Wilhelm Pieck, the Chairman of the SED, pointed out that once a West German state was set up, the Soviet Zone would inevitably have to

> develop its own independent state structure. It did not matter whether the Western Powers tore Germany apart . . . a month earlier or a month later. The important thing was to be prepared for every eventuality.

By March 1949 the SED was ready for this 'eventuality'. The constitution of the future East German state had been drafted and approved by the People's Council. On paper at least, it did not seem to be so very different from West Germany's, yet in reality, it was but a 'make-believe constitution'[8] camouflaging a one party dictatorship. In May a new People's Congress was elected. The voters, as in the other Soviet dominated countries in Eastern Europe, had been presented with just one list of candidates all of whom represented the views of the Socialist Unity Party (SED).

At the end of May the Congress met and approved the draft constitution, but Moscow kept the SED in suspense. The Soviets believed that there was still a slim chance of stopping the setting up of the FRG, but once the West German elections, in which the KPD won only 5.7 per cent of the voters, had taken place in August, there was no alternative to forming the German Democratic Republic (GDR), even though for the Soviets it was an exercise in damage limitation. On 12 October the government of the new state was formed and the Soviet military occupation of the Zone came to an end, although a Soviet Control Commission was set up, which, like the Allied High Commission in the West, retained considerable reserve powers.

c) Berlin

The division of Germany ensured that Berlin remained a divided city within a divided state within a divided continent. At the end of November 1948 the Germans in West Berlin, in response to threats and intimidation from the SED, set up their own city government with an elected assembly, which had an overwhelming anti-Communist majority. Britain, France and the USA permitted West Berlin to send representatives to sit in the West German parliament in Bonn, but, as the city was still legally under Four Power control, they had no voting rights. There was as yet no physical barrier between East and West Berlin, although the Soviet sector became the capital of the new GDR.

8 Assessment

> **KEY ISSUE** Was the division of Europe and Germany inevitable in 1948–9?

In the Autumn of 1947 the USA had hoped that it could through economic assistance alone set up a strong but friendly Western Europe that would be able to withstand pressure from the Soviet bloc. American officials believed that a strong economically and politically integrated Western Europe could also act as a magnet that would pull the Soviet satellites out of Moscow's orbit. By the Spring of 1948 it was clear that European economic integration was not happening. Military and economic weakness and the reluctance of Britain and France to go too far down the road of integration meant that the West

Europeans desperately needed assurances of American military support. The American presence was also the key to persuading France and the Benelux states that they had nothing to fear from a revived West Germany.

The more the USA was drawn into establishing in Western Europe what Geir Lundestad has called an 'empire by invitation',[9] the more it provoked Soviet reaction and the consolidation of the Soviet bloc, without, of course Yugoslavia. The Prague coup appeared to confirm all the West's worst fears about the USSR, and was an important factor leading to the decision to create West Germany and negotiate the North Atlantic Treaty. Stalin's unsuccessful attempt to force the Western Allies to drop their plans for West Germany by blockading West Berlin merely accelerated the division of Germany and left him with no option but to form an East German state.

With hindsight the division of Germany and Europe seems inevitable. Yet for Stalin the creation of a potentially independent West German state was a serious blow. East Germany has been described by Willy Loth as his 'unwanted child'.[10] Until his death he saw the GDR as only a temporary structure which he would be happy to dismantle, if he could somehow create a neutral Germany independent of an American dominated western Europe. By moving so quickly to set up a separate West Germany and a North Atlantic security system, were Britain, France and America responsible for the partition of Europe into two blocs? The eminent American diplomat, George Kennan, warned in September 1948 that this policy would lead to

> ... an irrevocable congealment of the division of Europe into two military zones: a Soviet zone and a US zone. Instead of the ability to divest ourselves gradually of the basic responsibility for the security of Western Europe, we will get a legal perpetuation of that responsibility.

In Britain, too, there were critical voices. In July 1948 General Robertson, the British Military Governor in Germany, in a memorandum to Bevin suggested that while

> 1 It would be impossible for the Western Allies to concede total evacuation because once British and US troops left Germany, the Soviets would have the country at their mercy. There is no reason, however, why the armed forces of the Allies should not withdraw into given fron-
> 5 tier areas, leaving Berlin and the main part of Germany to a single central government after which a peace treaty should be made on the analogy of the position immediately after [the Treaty of] Versailles. It would be essential that freedom of movement throughout the country should be guaranteed.

From the reaction to this advice in London, Paris and Washington it was obvious that most Western Europeans and their governments preferred a divided Germany and a West Europe protected by an American military presence to the uncertainties and risks which a neutral unified Germany would have exposed them to. It was by no means clear that Stalin would in reality have tolerated a genuine independent and neutral Germany.

References

1 T.P. Ireland, *Creating the Entangling Alliance: The Origins of the North Atlantic Allliance* (Aldwych Press, 1981), p. 64.
2 Michael Hogan, *The Marshall Plan* (CUP, 1987), p. 89.
3 L.I. Gibianskii, 'The Soviet–Yugoslav Conflict and the Soviet Bloc' in F. Gori and S. Pons (eds), *The Soviet Union and Europe in the Cold War, 1945–63* (Macmillan, 1996), p. 224.
4 *Ibid.*, p. 237.
5 Avi Schlaim, 'Britain, the Berlin Blockade and the Cold War', *International Affairs*, pp. 1–14 (Winter, 1984), p. 4.
6 Ireland, *op.cit.*, pp. 111–2.
7 N.M. Naimark, *The Russians in Germany: A History of the Soviet Zone of Occupation, 1945–50* (Harvard UP, 1995), p. 58.
8 P. Merkl, *The Origins of the West German Republic* (OUP, 1963), p. 175.
9 G. Lundestad, 'Empire by Invitation? The United States and Western Europe, 1945–52', *Journal of Peace Research*, vol. 23 (Sept 1986), pp. 263–77.
10 W. Loth, *Stalin's Unwanted Child: the Soviet Union, the German Question and the Founding of the GDR* (Macmillan, 1998).

Summary Diagram
The Division of Germany 1948–1949

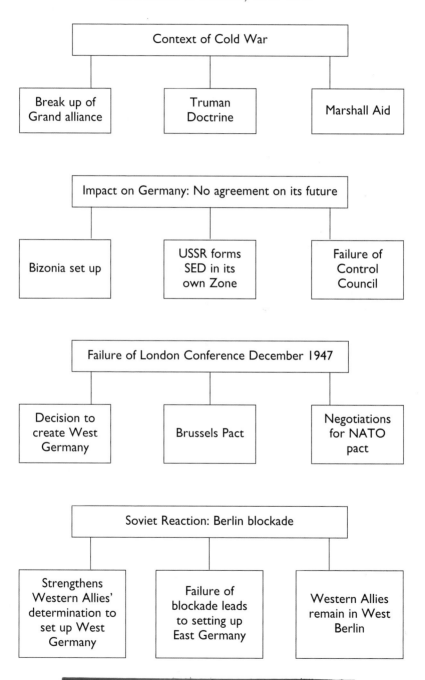

Working on Chapter 4

It is important that you understand this chapter as it contains the key events that mark the start of the Cold War: the breakdown of the London Foreign Ministers' Conference in December 1947, the division of Germany, the Berlin blockade, the signing of the Brussels treaty and then the setting up of the North Atlantic Treaty Organisation (NATO), as well as the consolidation of the Soviet bloc and the tensions between Belgrade and Moscow. In outline the political pattern for Europe had been set for the next 40 years. Therefore, as you work through this chapter, use the diagram and the subtitles to give you a structure for your notes. Make sure that you note clearly the process by which Europe and Germany were divided in 1948–9. Also while doing this, make a brief assessment of what caused the partition. Was it, as Western politicians argued in the 1950s, the fault of the USSR, or, as the revisionist historians insisted in the 1960s, the consequences of the economic imperialism of the USA? Perhaps, on the other hand, it was a vicious circle set in motion by all sorts of different factors? To answer these questions you will sometimes have to look back to chapters 2 and 3.

Answering structured questions on Chapter 4

In this chapter you have looked at the complex events that led to the division of Europe into the Soviet and Western blocs. When preparing to answer structured questions on this topic, it is important that you understand both why such events as the Prague coup or the Berlin blockade took place and what their consequences were. Remember that there will be two different types of question: factual questions, which will test your knowledge, and more analytical ones, which will require you to reflect on causes and consequences and the real reasons why certain key events occurred. Typical examples of structured questions are:

I. a) Outline briefly the events that led to the Berlin blockade.
  b) Describe how the Western Powers responded to the Berlin blockade.
  c) Could the Division of Germany have been avoided in 1949?

Questions 1a) and b) require essentially factual answers, but even so, you need to think carefully about what information you will draw on to answer them fully. In a) you will have to show how by December 1947 the former wartime allies had reached deadlock over Germany and that consequently the Western Powers decided to move ahead with building up a West German state. The Soviets responded by blockading West Berlin in the hope that this would force the Western Powers to give up their plans for a West Germany. In question b) you will need to explain how Britain and America organised the airlift, but that is not the whole story. You will also need to mention that the USA stationed 60 B29s in East Anglia and that the blockade merely intensified the efforts of the Western Allies to press on with setting up Western Germany and negotiating the North Atlantic Treaty.

Question c) is a broader and more analytical question. If you simply tell the story of *how* partition occurred, you will not get very many marks. You must explain and give your opinion about *why* it happened, drawing on the evidence from the last two chapters. You will need therefore to refer to Allied disagreements over reparation payments, the threatening ambiguity of the USSR's German policy as instanced by the creation of the SED, the formation of Bizonia and then the impact of the Marshall Plan, which all contributed to the failure of the London Foreign Ministers Conference in December 1947. Then the momentum towards division was accelerated by the shock of the Prague coup, which seemed to show that Western Europe was threatened by Soviet aggression. This led to the signature of the Brussels and North Atlantic Treaties, but, even more importantly, to plans for going ahead with constructing a new West German state. The Berlin blockade and its successful defeat by the Western Allies merely confirmed in Western eyes the correctness of their policy, while forcing the Soviets to create the GDR as a counterweight to the FRG. As long you are sure of your evidence in this type of question, do not be at all afraid to express your *own* opinions clearly. You may well agree with George Kennan and General Robertson that there were alternatives to the partition of Germany. On the other hand you might wish to stress that the vulnerability of West Europe to Soviet pressure and the ever present fear in France of a revived Germany made the partition of Germany and the creation of a Western European-American military bloc the only viable policy at the time.

Source-based questions on Chapter 4

Read the extracts from Stalin's statement at the meeting with the Western ambassadors on 2 August (pages 61–2) and the Soviet memorandum on the Berlin crisis (page 62), and look at the photo on page 62 and the diagram on page 63.

1 The Berlin Blockade
Read the extracts on pages 61–2 and look at the photograph on page 62 and the diagram on page 63.

a) Study the extract on pages 61–2.
 Use your own knowledge to explain what Stalin meant by '… restrictive measures under discussion' (lines 3–4). (5 marks)
b) Study the two extracts (pages 61–2).

i) What was the 'special currency' mentioned by Stalin (page 61, line 1)? (*2 marks*)

ii) Why did Stalin want it withdrawn from Berlin? (*3 marks*).

c) In what ways do these two extracts explain the reasons for the Berlin blockade? Explain your answer fully with reference to the above sources and to your own knowledge. (*7 marks*)

d) Look at the photograph on page 62 and the diagram on page 63. Of what value are these to the historian studying the reasons for the failure of the Berlin blockade? (*6 marks*)

2 Criticism of the Western Allied Policy on Germany
Read the two extracts on page 67.

a) Why does General Robertson argue that the Western Allies could not 'concede total evacuation' (extract 2, lines 1–2) of Germany to the Soviets? (*3 marks*)

b) What solution does Robertson suggest? (*4 marks*)

c) What does Kennan mean by 'an irrevocable congealment of the division of Europe' (extract 1, line 1)? (*3 marks*)

d) How far does Kennan support Robertson's arguments? (*5 marks*)

e) To what extent do these documents indicate that the Western Allies were responsible for the division of Germany? Explain your answer fully with reference to the above sources and your own knowledge. (*10 marks*)

Students often find source questions more difficult than essays. To answer them effectively you need both a wide ranging knowledge of the period as well as some quite specific skills. In most exam papers with source based questions your understanding of particular phrases and technical details quoted in the documents will be tested. Although the context of the document will certainly provide you with some information, you will also have to draw on your own knowledge to explain these details and phrases fully. Usually examiners include an illustration of some sort amongst the sources. If it is a photo, to interpret it properly you will again need to know the background of the events it has recorded. The key question to ask yourself before evaluating it, is what does it show and tell us about the past? Find out also when, where and why the photo was taken. Has the photographer created a mood or selected a viewpoint to make us particularly aware of something? Are the people in the photo posing or are they unaware of the camera? Could it have been edited? Is it propaganda? Remember that even if it is propaganda, it is still valuable to the historian because it shows what a government or political party wants people to believe.

5 The Consolidation of the Rival Blocs, 1950–55

POINTS TO CONSIDER

This chapter covers the period when Europe's division into two blocs appeared to have become a permanent fact of international life. As you read it, your objectives should be to understand in what way the Cold War was a major force behind the gathering pace of Western integration, how the USSR responded to the threat of an armed West Germany incorporated into the Western bloc and then, finally, what effect the death of Stalin had on East-West relations.

KEY DATES

1950	25 June	Outbreak of Korean War.
	24 Oct	French Assembly approve Pleven Plan.
1951	18 Apr	The European Coal and Steel Community (Schuman plan) Treaty signed.
1952	10 Mar	Stalin's note, proposing a neutral united Germany.
	27 May	EDC Treaty signed in Paris.
1953	5 Mar	Stalin dies.
	16–19 June	Strikes and riots in the GDR.
	July	Korean war ends.
1954	31 Aug	EDC rejected by the French Assembly.
1955	May	The FRG becomes a sovereign state and joins NATO.
		Warsaw Pact formed.
	20 Sept	USSR recognises sovereignty of GDR.

1 Western Integration, 1950–53

> **KEY ISSUES** Why did the Cold War make Western integration so necessary? What forms did Western Integration take 1950–53?

Despite the foundation of NATO in April 1949, there was a strong feeling in the Western Alliance in the winter of 1949–50 that the Soviet threat was growing. In September the USSR had successfully tested its first atom bomb, while a month later China fell to the Communists. Stalin also began to double the size of the Red Army. Meanwhile European integration was developing only slowly. NATO was still in its infancy and lingering fears of German domination amongst the Western European states stopped America from building up the new Federal Republic's (FRG) economic and military strength to a point where it could play a major role in the defence of Western Europe. Until the FRG was fully integrated into a Western European economic and military system there was a real danger that Stalin might be able to win the Germans over by offering them unity and markets stretching from the river Oder to the Pacific Ocean. At the same time American pressure to rearm West Germany and Truman's decision to develop the hydrogen bomb encouraged in Western Europe the emergence of a powerful peace movement, which Stalin immediately attempted to exploit.

a) The Schuman Plan

It was against this background that the Americans tried hard to find a formula that would overcome Western European fears of the growing economic power of the FRG and so enable the North Atlantic Alliance to benefit from its reserves of manpower and its industrial strength. The French came to realise that the only effective way of controlling the FRG was to integrate it firmly into a Western European economic and political union. But to make this work Britain would also have to join in order to balance the developing power of West Germany. Yet this solution was a non-starter because Britain refused to commit itself to further integration, and, instead, insisted on cultivating its special relationship with the USA and the Commonwealth. The alternative was to use NATO as a means of rearming West Germany and of aligning it firmly with the Western Powers within an Atlantic rather than Western European framework. By April 1950 the American Ambassador in Paris was urging

> an Atlantic Treaty Community that will comprise most of Western Europe as well as the US, UK and Canada and eventually Western Germany, that will function along political, military and economic lines.

The French still remained unconvinced. To them NATO was primarily a military alliance and they feared that within it West Germany would be able to develop its vast strength unchecked. They argued that the Americans and the British were subordinating the German problem to the Cold War, and that when it was over, France would once again be confronted with a strong Germany. To avoid this fate Schuman, the French Foreign Minister, announced in May 1950 a plan, devised by Jean Monnet, who was in charge of the French economic modernisation programme, to create the European Coal and Steel Community (ECSC). The Schuman Plan, as it was called, would enable the Western Allies to exploit Germany's coal and steel resources for their own rearmament programmes without running the risk of simultaneously building up a strong and independent West Germany. As far as the French were concerned, it was a substitute for German rearmament. It was received enthusiastically by Adenauer, the West German Chancellor, as he realised that only through integration could West Germany forge a partnership with the Western democracies and gain security from the USSR. Italy and the Benelux states also welcomed it, but Britain, not wishing to lose control of its own coal and steel industries, which the Labour Government had only just nationalised, did not. The French called a conference of the six states supporting the Plan in Paris in late summer 1950 to begin work on the nuts and the bolts of the scheme. Initially they intended to set firm limits on the amount of steel produced by the Germans, break up the great steel companies and end the ownership of the Ruhr coal mines by German industrialists, but the enormous demand for coal and steel caused by the outbreak of the Korean War strengthened Germany's negotiating position. In December the Americans had to intervene to force a compromise on both sides, which then enabled the Schuman Plan Treaty to be signed on 18 April 1951.

The ECSC replaced the International Ruhr Authority (see page 60) with a new supranational High Authority, which was controlled by the six member states. It regulated their coal and steel industries, guaranteeing that the economic needs of each member for these vital raw materials would be met. The Schuman Plan laid the foundations for Western European economic, and ultimately political, integration, and together with the NATO security umbrella, immeasurably strengthened the Western bloc. Michael Hogan argues that 'it amounted to the treaty of peace that had never been signed'[1] between Germany and France, as it went far towards removing the fears and animosities that had bedevilled European politics since 1870.

b) The Impact of the Korean War and the Problem of German Rearmament

The military planning staff in Washington advised Truman as early as 1947 to build up a West German army. The case for it became even stronger when the East Germans formed a strong paramilitary 'police force' in 1949. Behind the scenes Adenauer was already floating the idea that the FRG should contribute troops to 'an international legion', but politically West German rearmament remained a controversial issue. The prospect of it still alarmed the West European states, and the French argued that it would antagonise the USSR and trigger World War Three.

The Korean War changed the situation dramatically. The invasion of South Korea by North Korean troops on 25 June 1950 seemed to mark the start of a new global conflict in which the Soviets would finally overrun Western Europe. This impression was underlined when Ulbricht, the Secretary of the East German Politbureau, not only supported North Korean aggression but recommend similar action as a way of unifying Germany. In this context West German rearmament was inevitable. John McCloy, the American High Commissioner in the FRG, warned Truman on 18 July that:

1   If no means are held out for the Germans to fight in an emergency, my
    view is that we should probably lose Germany politically as well as mil-
    itarily without hope of regain. We should also lose, incidentally, a
    reserve of manpower which may become of great value in event of a
5   real war and could certainly be used by the Soviets against us.

c) The Proposed European Defence Community and the Spofford Compromise

The French were particularly anxious that Adenauer should not
exploit the need for West German troops to modify the Schuman Plan
and so allow the FRG's coal and steel industries to escape the restraints
of supranational control. Consequently, on Monnet's suggestion, the
French Prime minister, René Pleven, announced on 24 October the
so-called Pleven Plan, a proposal for a European 'Defence Community'. Essentially its purpose was to set up a European army under
supranational control, which would be linked to the ECSC. To ensure
that the FRG was kept on a tight rein its troops would join not in divisions (units of about 20,000 troops), but instead in battalions (much
smaller units composed of only about 800 troops).

Militarily the first version of the Pleven Plan was unworkable. It was
essentially a French plan aimed more at controlling German rearmament than at military effectiveness. The British refused to join and only
Belgium and Luxemburg showed any real interest, while the Americans
felt that it was a military nonsense. However, after prolonged discussions
in Washington a workable compromise was hammered out, which would
ultimately enable German troops to be recruited. Charles Spofford, the
deputy US representative on NATO's Atlantic Council, suggested that,
while the political problems caused by the EDC proposal were being
sorted out, certain practical steps to strengthen defences in Western
Europe 'upon which there already exist large measure of agreement'[2]
should be taken immediately. This was accepted at first by both France
and Britain and the other NATO members, and from this emerged the
Spofford Plan. This proposed that, while the EDC negotiations were
continuing, the West Germans would start to rearm and their troops,
tightly controlled by the Western Allies, would be integrated into NATO.
Eventually the Americans hoped to integrate the EDC into NATO,
thereby ensuring German membership of both organisations.

d) Strains Within the North Atlantic Alliance, December 1950–June 1951

At first it seemed as if the Spofford compromise had broken the deadlock over German rearmament. Preliminary negotiations about setting up the EDC began in Paris in February 1951, and at the same
time Adenauer began to discuss plans with the High Commissioners
for creating 12 divisions for NATO. The Western Powers also began

to normalise relations with the FRG. They officially terminated the state of war with Germany and opened negotiations to replace the Occupation Statute with a more appropriate treaty which recognised the FRG's new status.

Throughout the first half of 1951 the German rearmament question and American policy in Korea put an immense strain on the unity of the alliance. In Western Germany the Social Democrats bitterly attacked Adenauer's intention to join the EDC on the grounds that this would permanently divide Germany. He therefore attempted to drive a hard bargain with the Western Allies in order to convince his electorate that rearmament would lead to the FRG being given equality of treatment by its former occupiers. This, of course, frightened French public opinion, which would not allow their government to make any more concessions to the Germans.

The escalating conflict in Korea put further pressure on the Alliance. When Chinese troops came to the assistance of the North Koreans in November 1950, Western Europeans were alarmed by rumours that the Americans would retaliate by dropping nuclear bombs on China, and feared that this would lead to an all out war and the withdrawal of American troops from Europe. The British Prime Minister, Clement Attlee, with the support of the French Government, flew across to Washington to try to persuade the Americans to open negotiations with the Chinese. Truman refused on the grounds that he could not appease Communism in Asia while containing it in Europe, but he did reassure him that the atom bomb would not be used.

A month later relations between America and its Western allies were further strained by its plans to introduce a resolution in the United Nations condemning China as an aggressor and imposing a blockade on its trade. This again confronted the Western European statesmen with a dilemma: if they supported the resolution as it stood, they might be sucked into a large scale war in the Far East. On the other hand, if they did not, the USA might withdraw from Europe, leaving them facing a hostile USSR alone. Fortunately for the Western alliance the Americans toned down the resolution and its European allies were able to vote for it.

Once the Chinese sent troops into Korea, it was clear that the war would last a long time. This strengthened the hand of the Conservative Republican alliance in the US Congress, which forced Truman to make rearmament his Government's overriding priority. Marshall Aid was first diverted to defence support and then stopped altogether in favour of a military assistance programme. Inevitably this led to massive pressure on the Western European states to rearm more rapidly. The sheer expense of rearmament threatened to destabilise the North Atlantic Alliance at a time of acute danger. In Western Europe the NATO states increased their expenditure on rearmament from $4.4 billion in 1949 to $8 billion in 1951. This at first triggered a boom in industrial production, but because expensive raw materials such as coal, copper and rubber had to be imported in considerable quantities, it also caused inflation and serious balance of payments problems. Between July 1950 and June 1951 the cost of living increased by about 20 per cent in France and by about 10 per cent in Italy, the FRG and Britain. There was also increasing evidence that the shift in investment from civilian to military production and higher taxes was undermining political stability. In Britain a serious split developed in April in the Labour Cabinet over the cost of rearmament, while in the French and Italian elections of May and June 1951 both the Communists and the right-wing nationalist parties made a strong showing. In West Germany there were ominous signs that the extreme Right appeared to be making a comeback in the state elections in Lower Saxony.

It was no wonder then that Robert Marjolin, the Secretary-General of the Organisation for European Economic Cooperation (see page 57), was convinced that Western Europe was facing a great economic crisis, which could only be solved by a 'second Marshall Plan'. While it was unrealistic to expect any help on this scale from Washington, in July 1951 the OEEC and NATO did cooperate in a successful attempt to ensure that rearmament did not stifle the economic recovery of Western Europe. In August the OEEC called for a dramatic 25 per cent expansion of Western Europe's industrial production over the coming five years. It proposed financing both rearmament and domestic prosperity through increased production. In other words both guns and butter were to be produced! Thanks to the combination of the rearmament boom triggered by the Korean War and the steadily growing world demand for industrial goods and vehicles this proved a realistic plan. For the next 20 years Western Europe enjoyed a period of unparalleled prosperity, which in turn encouraged further economic and political integration and consolidated the Western bloc.

e) The Signature of the EDC and General Treaties, May 1952

Under American pressure detailed negotiations on the EDC started in Paris in October 1951. Simultaneously talks began in Bonn between the High Commissioners and Adenauer on replacing the Occupation Statute. Both sets of negotiations proved complicated and dragged on until May 1952. In Bonn the sticking point was how much independence the Western Allies were ready to give the FRG, and in Paris the key issue was still French determination to prevent Germany from becoming a major military power again. Thus the French vetoed German membership of NATO, despite the Spoffard Compromise (page 76), and continued jealously to restrict the size of German units that could be integrated into the EDC. It was only American pressure that finally forced the French government to sign the treaty in May 1952. After that there began the long struggle to have the treaty ratified by the national parliaments of France and West Germany.

2 Stalin's Attempts to Stop Western Rearmament and the Integration of the FRG into the EDC

> **KEY ISSUES** How did Stalin attempt to stop Western rearmament and why did he fail?

Stalin attempted to counter the threat of NATO and German rearmament in two ways. Firstly he tried to exploit fears in West Europe of a new world war by launching the Communist-led World Peace Movement, which campaigned for disarmament and world peace. More ambitiously he also attempted to stop West Germany's military and economic integration into Western Europe. From the Autumn of 1950 until the Spring of 1952 he put forward, either at international level or through the GDR, a series of initiatives aimed at achieving a united but neutral Germany. In March 1952 in a note to the Western Allies he made a far-reaching proposal for free elections, supervised by a commission of the four former occupying Powers, which would lead to the setting up of an independent Germany. The new reunified Germany would not be allowed to make alliances against former enemies, and so could hardly join the EDC, but, on the other hand, it would not be burdened with demands for reparations, denazification and for the socialisation of the economy. It would also be allowed to have its own limited armed forces. Was Stalin really serious about this offer? Many West Germans believed that Adenauer should have responded more positively to Stalin's initiative. They were convinced that it was a 'missed opportunity', an opinion that has been echoed by modern historians, of whom Steininger and Loth are the most persuasive.[3] Adenauer, however, like the Americans and the British, wanted to see the FRG firmly integrated into the West and not replaced by a unified neutral Germany, which would be vulnerable to Soviet pressure. Thus Stalin's initiative was never fully explored by the Western Powers. In July 1952 Ulbricht was given the go-ahead for an accelerated socialisation programme in East Germany, which suggested that Stalin had now finally given up the idea of sacrificing the GDR to stop the rearmament of the FRG.

3 Eastern Integration

> **KEY ISSUES** How did Stalin control Eastern Europe and how did Eastern 'integration' differ from Western integration?

On the surface the Soviet Bloc appeared stable, yet its unity was fragile. Unlike the West it was essentially held together by coercion, and had no international organisations comparable to NATO, the OEEC and the ECSC. The COMINFORM was set up to create ideological unity in Eastern Europe, but by 1949 it was rapidly lapsing into inactivity. Similarly the Council for Mutual Economic Assistance (COMECON), which was created to counter the Marshall Plan, was in reality just a 'paper organization until the late 1950s'.[4] The only effective ties strengthening the Bloc were the network of bilateral treaties 'of friendship, cooperation and mutual assistance' signed between the USSR and the satellite states and also between these states themselves. Each of these treaties contained the following agreements:

- a mutual defence agreement;
- a ban on joining a hostile alliance such as NATO;
- recognition of equality, sovereignty and non-interference in each other's internal affairs (although in practice this did not deter the USSR from intervening in the domestic policies of its satellites).

There were also a series of interstate agreements covering economic, scientific and technical cooperation. Stalin achieved obedience to the Soviet line by frequently summoning the leaders of the Eastern bloc states to Moscow, and also through the direct participation of Soviet ambassadors and advisers in the internal affairs of the satellites. In the background, of course, there was always the threat of the Red Army. The armed forces of the satellite states, unlike the NATO armies, formed a completely integrated system centred on Moscow. Each army was issued with Soviet equipment, training manuals and armaments. Even the style of uniform was identical. The Stalin cult was also a unifying factor in the Eastern Bloc. He was celebrated everywhere as the builder of Socialism in the USSR and the liberator of Eastern Europe. To survive in this period local politicians had to be 'more like Stalin than Stalin himself',[5] and their societies and economies had to be based on the Soviet model. Farms were collectivised, central planning for the economy was introduced and heavy industry was to be developed in a series of five year plans.

4 Western Attempts to Destabilise the Soviet Bloc

KEY ISSUE How did the West try to destabilise the Soviet bloc in the period 1949–52?

To the Americans, Tito's break with the Kremlin in 1948 indicated how fragile the unity of the Soviet bloc was. Secretly, so as not to discredit Tito in the eyes of his fellow Communists, Truman granted

Yugoslavia economic and military assistance. Between 1949 and 1952 there were also a series of unsuccessful operations planned by the Americans and British involving landing agents and paramilitary forces in Albania to overthrow the Communist government of Enver Hoxha. Attempts were also made to undermine Soviet power in the other satellite states by complaining in the United Nations about human rights abuses in the ex-Axis states of Romania, Bulgaria and Hungary with which the Western Allies had signed peace treaties in 1947. The West also restricted trade with the satellite states, so that they would be forced to look to the USSR for goods, which it could only supply at considerable cost to itself. Eastern European refugees were subsidised, as was *Radio Free Europe*, which broadcast anti-Soviet propaganda to the states behind the Iron Curtain. All these measures were aimed at weakening Soviet power in Eastern Europe over the long-term. The USA and its allies was not ready to risk war with the USSR, especially as it was now a nuclear power.

5 Leadership Changes in the USA and USSR and Their Impact on the Cold War

> **KEY ISSUE** What impact did the new leaders in the USA and USSR have on the Cold War?

In November 1952 Eisenhower, standing as a Republican, won the American Presidential election. During the election campaign there had been much talk about 'rolling back the frontiers of Communism', but, like his predecessor, he was not ready to risk war, and privately he expressed considerable doubts 'about how much we should poke at the animal through the bars of the cage'.[6] Western military integration and support for Adenauer remained the cornerstone of American policy in Europe.

In March 1953 Stalin's death also led to changes in the Soviet leadership. His one-man dictatorship was replaced by a collective leadership composed of Malenkov, Khrushchev, Molotov, Bulganin and, for a short time, Beria. At home this group was determined to improve living standards and cautiously to dismantle the apparatus of terror created by Stalin. To carry out these reforms they needed a more relaxed international climate. Shortly after Stalins's death Malenkov declared in the Supreme Soviet:

> At the present time there is no disputed or unresolved question that cannot be settled by mutual agreement of the interested countries. This applies to our relations with all states, including the United States of America.

Given this new peace offensive by the Soviet leadership, it looked briefly as if the German question might be reopened. The obvious dangers in this for the North Atlantic Alliance was that it would slow up the progress of Western military integration, give the French assembly an excuse not to ratify the EDC Treaty and weaken the position of Adenauer. Eisenhower therefore responded cautiously and on 16 April announced that any improvement in Soviet-American relations was dependent on free elections in Eastern Europe. In May Churchill, who had won the British general election in October 1951, suggested a four power conference. This proposal was unpopular with both Adenauer and Eisenhower who feared that it might reopen the German question, but such was the desire for peace throughout Western Europe, particularly in the FRG, that both statesmen reluctantly had to agree to discuss a possible agenda for talks at a preliminary Western summit, although this did not meet until December in Bermuda.

6 The East German Riots, June 1953

KEY ISSUES Why did the revolt break out and what were its international consequences?

In the Spring on 1953 Beria, the Deputy Soviet Prime Minister, urged his colleagues to sell the GDR to West Germany for the payment of 10 billion dollars since it was proving an expensive and potentially unstable state to keep going. Ulbricht's programme of forced collectivisation of farms and of socialisation was causing a mass exodus of East Germans fleeing westwards through the open frontier in Berlin. Although Beria failed to convince his colleagues, who still clung to the idea of working slowly and cautiously towards a unified Socialist Germany, Ulbricht was ordered to pursue a more conciliatory approach in East Germany and to abandon his programme for rapid socialisation. These concessions were made too late and also failed to scale down the high production targets, which had been set for the workers by Ulbricht. A series of strikes and riots broke out throughout East Germany on 16 June. At the request of the East German government Soviet troops backed by tanks intervened on 17 June to suppress them. Sporadic demonstrations and riots then continued throughout the Summer.

The uprising took both the Soviets and the Western powers by surprise, and has been called by Christian Ostermann 'one of the most significant focal points in the history of the Cold War'.[7] The American Government at first welcomed the crisis, as it upset the whole Soviet peace offensive and made the calling of a Four Power conference much less likely. For this very reason Churchill tried to play down Soviet intervention and stressed, correctly in fact, that Soviet troops had acted with considerable restraint. The Americans, on the other hand, hoped that the sight of Soviet troops on the

An East Berlin Communist official is being taken into protective custody by West Berlin police after fleeing from rioters in East Berlin, 19 June 1953.

streets of East Berlin would fuel West German fears of the USSR and persuade the voters to re-elect Adenauer in the September election. Yet there was a considerable danger that, if the USA was seen to do nothing to help the East Germans, there could, as one American official said, 'be a terrible let down in East and West Germany, which will seriously affect the American position and even more seriously affect Adenauer's position'.[8] Eisenhower's advisers therefore came up with a two-pronged strategy. The USA would respond to pressure from public opinion in West Germany for international intervention to help the East Germans by calling for a four power foreign ministers conference on the future of Germany, but at the same time, through provocative broadcasts from its radio stations in West Berlin, it would do all it could to prolong the unrest in East Germany.

This policy certainly strengthened support for Adenauer in the FRG, who duly won the election in September with a greatly increased vote; but it also made it much more difficult for the Soviets to make any real concessions on the status of the GDR. The revolt led not only to Beria's arrest and execution on the orders of his political rivals, but also to a re-think of Soviet policy towards the GDR. The unpopularity of the Socialist Unity Party (SED) in East Germany and the hatred for the Communists in the FRG forced the Soviets to come to the conclusion that the prospect of a friendly united neutral Germany was unrealistic and that therefore they had little option but to concentrate on consolidating the GDR.

7 The Collapse of the EDC and West Germany Joins NATO

KEY ISSUE Why did the French finally reject the EDC, but allow the FRG to join NATO?

On 15 May 1953 the EDC and the General Treaty were at last ratified by the West German Parliament, but only after prolonged opposition from the Social Democrats. Soviet intervention in East Germany on June 17 was then seen by most West Germans as a confirmation that Adenauer's policy of joining the EDC was correct. In France, however, the situation was very different. The French began to have second thoughts about the EDC almost as soon as they had signed it, and their Government adopted the tactics of dragging out the ratification process as long as possible. Stalin's death, the end of the Korean war in July 1953 and the Soviet peace offensive all appeared to have made the EDC less necessary. Finally, after failing to gain major changes in the Treaty the French Chamber rejected it on 30 August 1954. Two years earlier such a defeat would have led to Adenauer's resignation and most likely to renewed Franco-German rivalry, which would have fatally undermined the unity of Western Europe. By 1954, however, Adenauer's position was immeasurably stronger. He had won the 1953 election, the economy of the FRG was booming and he enjoyed the support of the new American Secretary of State, John Foster Dulles. The French, on the other hand, were weakened by their defeat in Indo-China where they had been waging since 1945 a bitter colonial war, and were therefore vulnerable to Anglo-American pressure.

The immediate priorities of the British and Americans were to secure the FRG's entry into NATO. French fears of a rearmed Germany were overcome by Adenauer's agreement to limit the Federal army to the size envisaged in the EDC Treaty, his voluntarily renouncement of nuclear weapons and Britain's commitment permanently to keep four divisions supported by air power on the Continent. In October 1954 a fresh settlement was hammered out which recognised the sovereignty of the Federal Republic and its membership of NATO. Britain, as well as the six states that had initially been members of the EDC joined a new non-supranational organisation, the Western European Union, which formed a strong European grouping within NATO. The Western Allies again committed themselves to work towards a united federal Germany integrated into a democratic Western Europe. Until this happened their troops would remain in the FRG, and Berlin would still be under four Power control. On 5

Chancellor Adenauer addressing the first batch of volunteers for the new West German army in January 1956.

May 1955 the Treaty came into force and four days later the FRG, joined NATO.

These treaties effectively completed the post-war settlement of Western Europe. The German historian, Hans-Peter Schwarz, has compared them to the Vienna Settlement of 1815, which created a generation of peace after the Napoleonic wars. Yet they also deepened the division of Europe. While theoretically the door was kept open for German unification, in reality the integration of the FRG into NATO made unity in the foreseeable future unlikely. The very success of Western integration intensified what Christoph Klessmann has called 'the reactive mechanism'[9] of the Cold War: the more the FRG was integrated into the West, the more tightly bound was the GDR into the Soviet bloc.

8 The Warsaw Pact Treaty

KEY ISSUE To what extent was the Warsaw Pact the consequence of West Germany's membership of NATO?

The Soviets reacted 'surprisingly mildly'[10] to West Germany's membership of NATO and did not let it interfere with their plans for the coming Geneva Conference (see page 87). Nevertheless, on 14 May the USSR and the Eastern European states signed the Warsaw Pact, which the GDR eventually joined in January 1956. The introduction to the Treaty clearly stated that the main reason for its signature was:

I   ... the situation created in Europe by the ratification of the Paris agreements, which envisage the formation of a new military alignment in the shape of 'Western European Union', with the participation of a re-militarized Western Germany and the integration of
5   the latter in the North Atlantic *bloc*, which increases the danger of another war and constitutes a threat to the national security of peacable states.

The pact committed its members to consult on issues of mutual interest and to give all necessary assistance in the event of an attack on any one of them in Europe. Essentially it was a political statement rather than an effective military alliance, as it lacked organisation and for its first few years was 'little more than a shell'.[11] The treaty still kept open the option of a neutral Germany by declaring that if a 'general European treaty of Collective security' was signed, the Warsaw Pact would lapse.

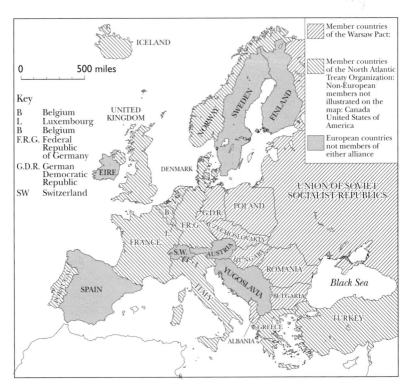

NATO and the Warsaw Pact, 1956

9 The Geneva Conference, July 1955

> **KEY ISSUE** What significance, if any, did the Geneva Conference have?

By the Summer of 1955 the Cold War had reached a stage of equilibrium. Increasingly the nuclear weapons possessed by the two Superpowers, the USA and USSR, appeared to rule out war and make peaceful coexistence the only practical option. In May the Soviets agreed to evacuate Austria provided it remained neutral, and in July the leaders of Britain, France, the USA and USSR met for the first time since Potsdam at Geneva. Here, however the limits to the new spirit of coexistence, or *détente*, were quickly reached. No agreement was achieved on the future of Germany or on disarmament, but at least conversations were conducted in an atmosphere of friendship and the division of Europe was treated as a diplomatic fact of life.

In September Adenauer visited Moscow to negotiate the return of the last German prisoners of war and to establish normal diplomatic relations with the USSR. Far from leading to a breakthrough in the German question the division between the two Germanies widened still further. To reassure East Germany of continued Soviet support Nikita Khrushchev acknowledged the GDR as an independent state in its own right. Adenauer, worried that an exchange of ambassadors with the USSR might be interpreted to mean that his government recognised the legal existence of the GDR, immediately announced the Hallstein Doctrine (named after an official who had helped formulate it). This stated that the FRG would consider the recognition of the GDR by any state, other than the USSR, as an unfriendly act which would lead to an immediate break in diplomatic relations. The Hallstein doctrine showed clearly the limits to the 'Geneva spirit'.

10 Assessment

> **KEY ISSUE** Why was the German question such an important issue in the 'First Cold War'?

During those tense and anxious years from the end of the Berlin blockade in 1949 to the death of Stalin in 1953 the crucial issue that dominated the Cold War in Europe was the future of Germany. Whoever controlled Germany would dominate Europe. The Western Powers were therefore determined not to risk the creation of a neutral Germany, which could easily be influenced by the USSR or might indeed seek to play off Moscow against Washington. They did, after all, control two thirds of postwar Germany in which the Ruhr, the biggest industrial centre in the world, was situated. Were war to break out with the USSR, it was clear to the military planners in NATO that West German industrial resources and soldiers would be needed, if there was to be any chance of halting a Soviet military advance before it reached the Rhine. French fears of even a revived West Germany had to be overcome in the interests of the Atlantic Alliance as a whole. This was the key to the tortuous negotiations over the EDC, which dragged on from late 1950 to August 1954.

The prospect of an armed West Germany also alarmed Stalin, who attempted to neutralise the FRG by all means short of war. He cleverly tried to exploit the strong West German passivist movement in 1950–51, and in 1952 appeared to hold out the prospect of German re-unification provided Adenauer pulled out of the EDC talks. Perhaps Stalin's offer was genuine, but the Western Powers could not afford to take a risk on the future of Germany. Yet by 1954 the USA and USSR were edging towards what the diplomats call a *modus vivendi* (an agreement to tolerate each other's position) on the German question. Although the Americans had exploited Soviet difficulties in the GDR during the riots and strikes of June–July 1953, they had nevertheless respected the GDR as a Soviet sphere of influence and carefully avoided sending in troops. Similarly when the FRG joined NATO, the USSR no longer saw its membership as a danger that had to be averted at all costs. It did, of course, respond by forming the Warsaw Pact. Although this was of more political than military significance, it did mark the final consolidation of Europe into two blocs.

References

1 M. Hogan, *The Marshall Plan* (CUP, 1987), p. 378.
2 T.P. Ireland, *Creating the Entangling Alliance: The Origins of the North Atlantic Treaty Organization* (Aldwych Press, 1981), p. 205.
3 W. Loth, *Stalin's Unwanted Child: The Soviet Union, the German Question and the Founding of the GDR* (Macmillan, 1998); R. Steininger, *The German Question, the Stalin Note of 1952 and the Problem of Reunification* (Columbia UP, 1990).
4 R.L. Hutchings, *Soviet–East European Relations: Consolidation and Conflict, 1968–1980* (University of Wisconsin Press, Madison, 1983), p. 16.
5 *Ibid.*, p. 18.
6 J. Gaddis, *The Long Peace* (OUP, New York, 1987), p. 177.
7 C.F. Ostermann, 'The United States and the East German Uprising of 1953 and the Limits of Rollback', *Cold War International History Project, Working Paper, no. 11* (Woodrow Wilson International Center for Scholars, Washington, DC, Dec. 1994), p. 2 on the Internet at cwihp.si.edu, p. 9.
8 *Ibid.*, p. 22.
9 Quoted in D.G. Williamson, *Germany from Defeat to Partition* (Pearson, 2001), p. 42.
10 W. Gaddis, *We Now Know* (Oxford, 1997), p. 135.
11 Hutchings, *op.cit.*, p. 22.

Summary Diagram
The Consolidation of the Two Blocs

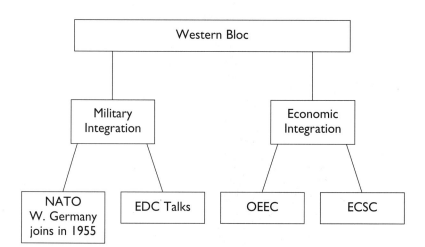

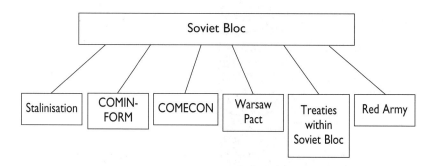

Working on Chapter 5

This chapter focuses on the importance of the German question in the 'First Cold War' and on the consolidation of the two rival blocs. Your notes should concentrate first of all on picking out the key developments in the complex question of German rearmament. You must show why the outbreak of the Korean war made West German rearmament so vital, how the French devised the EDC only to reject it in 1954, and why Stalin was unsuccessful in stopping attempts to rearm the FRG. When you have finished this, go on to look at the impact of the first Cold war on the two blocs and how both sides attempted to use all means short of war to undermine each other. Why do you think that it can be argued that the First Cold War ended with the death of Stalin? Finally with the help of the summary diagram show how and why the two Cold War blocs had become consolidated by 1955.

Answering structured and essay questions on Chapter 5

1. a) Describe the impact of the Korean War on Western Europe, 1950–51.
  b) What was the Schuman Plan and how did it help integrate West Germany into the Western Bloc?
  c) Why did France never ratify the EDC Treaty? Why were the consequences in 1954 less serious for the Western Powers than they might have been two years earlier?
2. a) Outline how Stalin attempted to stop West German rearmament.
  b) Why was the Soviet Note of March 1952 unsuccessful in creating a neutral Germany?
  c) What consequences for the German question did the East German riots of 17 June have?

In 1a) the whole question of German rearmament is vital, but look also at the economic and social consequences of the rearmament programmes right across Western Europe and the rise of the peace movement. Point out how these strained relations with the USA, and that when China came into the war in November 1950, there was a danger that the USA would become bogged down in a major struggle that might distract it from defending Western Europe. In 1b) you need to explain how the Schuman Plan by removing Franco-German economic rivalry was brilliantly successful in strengthening the Western Bloc. 1c) requires more analysis that the other two questions. Why, unlike the Schuman plan, was the EDC rejected by the French Parliament? It is true, of course, that the French deeply disliked the prospect of German rearmament, yet that is only part of the answer. You need to point out that Britain's refusal to join made it potentially harder for the French to balance German power within the EDC and that by August 1954 it was safe to reject the EDC, as the USSR was obviously interested in stabilising the situation in Europe. This last point is relevant for explaining why the collapse of the EDC did not seriously weaken the West. By 1954 the FRG was economically stable and had proved a loyal member of the ECSC. A year after having intervened in East Germany to crush the East German riots, the USSR had no way of persuading the West Germans to opt for a neutral united Germany. You will also need to look at how quickly Britain and America moved to faciltate the FRG's entry into NATO and how Adenauer himself tried to meet French fears by voluntarily renouncing atomic weapons.

In question 2a) look at how Stalin aimed at exploiting the fear of war amongst the Western European peoples, especially the Germans, whilst also trying through diplomatic means to secure a united pro-Soviet Germany. The Stalin Note (2b) was part of this offensive. Did it fail because the Western Powers had every reason to suspect its motives? Was there any evidence that Stalin would have tolerated a genuinely neutral unified Germany? 2c) is a rather more difficult question. You may come to the conclusion that it had little real impact as the Western Powers were not ready to intervene. On the other hand before the riots of 17 June pressure was building up throughout Europe for a fresh look at the German question. Without it might Beria have survived and found the Western Powers receptive to his ideal of 'selling' the GDR? Ask yourself particularly what the consequences were of the intervention of Soviet troops in East Germany.

Structured questions tend to focus more narrowly on topics. Essay questions are more wide-ranging. Consider, for instance, this title:

> To what extent had Stalin's European policy been shown to be a failure by the time of his death?

Ask yourself initially what the question actually means and what information you need to draw on to answer it. Examiners often use the words 'to what extent'. They indicate that you must make some sort of judgement or evaluation. Thus before you can assess whether or not Stalin's European policy was a failure, you must be sure what his European policy was. Look back over your notes of the last five chapters and work out how you will plan out your essay. Each paragraph should deal with an important argument that explores and answers a particular aspect of the question. In the introduction summarise the main thrust of your arguments and clarify any obscure points in the question. Could it be that in some areas, such as the role played by the Communist Parties in Western Europe, Stalin's policy had failed by 1953? Similarly his attempts to create a pro-Soviet Germany, or at the very least to stop the integration of Western Germany into an American dominated Western bloc, had also very obviously failed by his death. On the other hand he had created a ring of satellite states in Eastern Europe and made the USSR the greatest military power in Europe. As with most historical problems, it is likely that you will conclude that there is no clear cut answer: Stalin's European policy was a failure in some areas and a success in others. As you write out your essay do not lapse into narrative. *Your task is to argue relevantly and to answer the question set.*

Source-based questions on Chapter 5

1 *The Korean War and German Rearmament*

Read the extracts on page 74 from the US Ambassador in Paris and on page 76 from McCloy, the US High Commissioner, in Bonn.

a) i) Explain what the Ambassador means by an 'Atlantic Treaty Community' (page 74, line 1). (*3 marks*)

ii) Explain what McCloy means by 'emergency' (page 76, line 1). (*3 marks*)

b) Why does McCloy think that without rearmament Germany might be 'politically as well as militarily' lost to the West (page 76, lines 2–3)? (*5 marks*)

c) To what extent do these extracts and any other evidence known to you explain American and Western European attitudes towards German rearmament, 1950–55? (*10 marks*)

2 *The Warsaw Pact*

Read the extract on page 86 from the Warsaw Pact Treaty and look at the photograph on page 85 and the map on page 86.

a) Explain what is meant by the 'situation created in Europe' (page 86, line 1). (*3 marks*)

b) Why did the Soviets think that this 'situation' increased the danger of 'another war' (line 6)? (*5 marks*)

c) How far was the Warsaw Pact an exercise in damage limitation by the USSR? Using this extract, photo and your own knowledge explain your answer fully. (*5 marks*)

d) Using this extract, photo, map and your own knowledge, explain how the signature of the Warsaw Pact completed the consolidation of Europe into two blocs. (*7 marks*)

6 The Khrushchev Era and the 'Second Cold War', 1956–63

POINTS TO CONSIDER

This chapter focuses upon the eventful period when Khrushchev was trying both to consolidate the USSR's grip on Eastern Europe, whilst also attempting to 'destalinise', or liberalise, conditions within it. Note carefully what the consequences of these policies were for the development of the Cold War. The second half of the chapter analyses the long Berlin crisis of 1958–61. As you read these sections, ask yourself why this period is sometimes regarded as the 'Second Cold War'.

KEY DATES

1956	25 Feb	Khrushchev attacks Stalin at 20th Party Congress.
	June	Riots in Poland.
	23 Oct–4 Nov	Hungarian uprising defeated.
1957	25 Mar	Treaty of Rome signed.
1958	27 Nov	Khrushchev's Berlin ultimatum.
1960	16–17 May	Paris Summit breaks down.
1961	13 Aug	Berlin Wall built.
1962	Oct	Cuban Crisis.

1 The Year of Crises: 1956

> **KEY ISSUES** Why did destalinisation cause serious crises within the Soviet bloc and what were the international consequences of these crises?

a) Destalinisation

Destalinisation had a big impact on the relations between the USSR and its satellite states. It appeared to promise a return to the policy of 'different roads to socialism', which Stalin briefly tolerated between 1945 and 1947 (see pages 45–6). The first stage of destalinisation occurred with the fall of Beria. His secret police network, which had spies throughout Eastern Europe, was dissolved and politicians like Gomulka in Poland and Kadar in Hungary were released from prison and returned to public life. This raised expectations in the satellite states that they would be given more independence from Moscow.

The second wave of destalinisation followed after Khrushchev's famous speech at the 20th. Party Conference in February 1956

KHRUSHCHEV 1894–1971

In 1938 Nikita Khrushchev became First Secretary of the Communist Party in the Ukraine. A year later he joined the USSR's Politbureau. After Stalin's death he was appointed to the influential position of First Secretary of the Soviet Communist party. By the time the 20th Party Congress met in February 1956 he was already the most powerful figure in the USSR. He was convinced that Communism would eventually win the economic and ideological competition with capitalism. Although this competition was to be peaceful, he did not hesitate to play on the West's fear of nuclear war to achieve his ends. His opportunism and 'nuclear sabre rattling'[1] made the world a much more dangerous place than it had been in Stalin's time.

denouncing Stalin and recognising the right of the satellite states to find their 'national ways to socialism'. Although the speech was supposed to be secret, the American Security service, the CIA, acquired a copy and ensured that it was broadcast to Eastern Europe. By raising hopes of political change this contributed to the unrest in Poland and Hungary later in the year. Expectations of reform were further increased by the improvement in relations between the USSR and Yugoslavia, which was 'readmitted' to the Socialist bloc after Khrushchev and Bulganin had visited Belgrade in May 1955, and attributed the blame for the break in 1948 fairly and squarely to Stalin (see page 59). Khrushchev was, of course, primarily interested in bringing back Yugoslavia into the Soviet sphere of influence, while Tito, the Yugoslav leader, ambitiously believed that, as a result of his experience in defying Stalin, he was a role model for the new generation of Soviet leaders and would now become a leading figure in the Soviet Bloc. In June 1956 after talks in Moscow Khrushchev and Tito issued a communiqué in which they agreed that

1   the path of socialist development differs in various countries and conditions, that the multiplicity of forms of socialist development tends to strengthen socialism and that any tendency of imposing one's opinions on the ways and forms of socialist development is alien to
5   both.

This was an optimistic doctrine assuming that the satellite states wished to remain within the Soviet bloc. What would happen, however, if one or more of these states decided to take a controversial road to socialism, with which the USSR did not agree? Would it intervene militarily or run the risk of seeing the Soviet bloc disintegrate?

b) The Polish Crisis and the Return of Gomulka, June–October 1956

The limits to this doctrine were tested first in Poland in the autumn of 1956. At the end of June riots broke out in Poznan when the local factory workers protested about the imposition of increased work targets. They were put down with heavy casualties, but to overcome the bitterness this caused, the Polish Communist Party turned again to its popular former leader, Gomulka (see page 58), who had just been released from prison. The Soviet government, fearing that he would seek to restore Polish independence, sent a high powered Delegation to Warsaw on 19–20 October, and ordered the Red Army units stationed in Poland to advance on the city in an attempt to stop his election. Gomulka refused to be cowed and his election went ahead. On 24 October Khrushchev told a Central Committee meeting in Moscow that

1 the discussions between the delegations ranged from being very warm to rude. Gomulka several times emphasised that they would not permit their independence to be taken away and would not allow anyone to interfere in Poland's internal affairs. He said that if he were leader of the
5 country he would restore order promptly.

Faced with the prospect of having to fight the Poles at a time when the situation in Hungary was rapidly deteriorating, Khrushchev wisely withdrew the troops and chose to believe Gomulka's assurances that Poland would remain a loyal member of the Warsaw Pact. As the Russian leader was to observe, 'finding a reason for an armed conflict now would be very easy, but finding a way to put an end to such a conflict would be very hard'.[2]

c) The Hungarian and Suez Crises

Just as the worst of the Polish crisis was over, the USSR was faced in Hungary with the most serious challenge to its power since the War. As part of his destalinisation campaign Khrushchev had, with Tito's backing, put pressure on the Hungarian Communist Party in July to replace its old-style Stalinist leader, Mátyás Rákosi, with the more liberal Ernö Gerö. Tito had considerable ambitions in Hungary, as he hoped that an independent Communist regime would emerge in Budapest, which would look to Belgrade rather than Moscow and so strengthen his overall influence within the Soviet bloc.

In the early Autumn the pressures for further change, which Tito encouraged, continued to grow. A turning point was reached on 23 October when a large demonstration in Budapest, called in support of the Polish reformers, escalated out of control. Even before he had received a formal request for help from Gerö, Khrushchev decided to send in 30,000 troops backed with tanks and artillery. A new government under Imre Nagy, who was an independent minded and reforming Communist, supported by Tito, was formed. Khrushchev at first tried to reconcile his pledges to concede greater independence to the satellite states with Soviet security needs. He issued on 30 October the 'Declaration on the Principles of Development and a Further Strengthening of Friendship and Cooperation between the USSR and other Socialist Countries', which attempted to provide a legal and mutually agreed framework for Soviet military bases in Eastern Europe. He also began to pull out the troops from Hungary, but then Nagy theatened the whole foundations of the USSR's power in Eastern Europe by announcing that he intended to withdraw Hungary from the Warsaw Pact. He was also planning to share power with non-Communist groups.

Soviet policy during the Hungarian uprising cannot be fully understood without also looking at the Suez crisis. The USSR had been so successful in cultivating good relations with Colonel Nasser, the Egyptian leader, that the Americans decided to bring him to heel by cancelling their loan for building the Aswan dam in July 1956. This merely prompted Nasser to turn to the USSR for finance and to nationalise the Suez Canal, which was owned by an Anglo-French company. Britain and France responded by drawing up a complex plan, which also involved an Israeli attack on Egypt, to topple Nasser and seize the Suez Canal. British planes began to bomb Egyptian airfields on 31 October, at the very time that the Hungarian crisis was reaching its peak. Khrushchev was convinced that Nasser would be quickly removed and that Soviet influence in the Middle East would suffer a disastrous blow. If this was combined with further set backs in Hungary, Soviet power and prestige might never recover. Consequently that same day he told the Central Committee of the USSR:

> We should reexamine our assessment and should not withdraw our
> 1 troops from Hungary and Budapest. We should take the initiative in
> restoring order in Hungary. If we depart from Hungary, it will give a
> great boost to the Americans, English and French – the imperialists.
> They will perceive it as a weakness on our part and will go on the offen-
> 5 sive. We would then be exposing the weakness of our positions. Our
> party will not accept it if we do this. To Egypt they will then add
> Hungary. We have no other choice....

On the 4 November Soviet troops advanced into Hungary and, after a few days of fierce fighting, a new government loyal to the USSR under János Kádár was installed. Khrushchev had nothing to fear from Western intervention. Eisenhower, suspecting that the USSR might be willing to risk war rather than lose Hungary, made it absolutely clear to the Soviet leaders that there was no question of American intervention to save Nagy. However, much to Khrushchev's surprise, Nasser was saved by the Americans, who viewed the Suez war as an attempt by Britain and France to prop up their disintegrating empires in the Middle East and Africa. Through massive diplomatic and financial

Russian officers in Budapest, November 1956, advance threateningly towards a Western photographer.

pressure on London and Paris Eisenhower managed to halt the fighting on 6 November just at the point where the British and French troops were near to capturing the whole length of the Suez Canal.

Khrushchev cleverly exploited this split in the Western Alliance and on 5 November threatened nuclear missile attacks on Britain, France and Israel if they did not stop the war. Although it was known at the time by Western intelligence that the USSR did not yet possess the rockets to propel such missiles, the ceasefire the following day made it look as if it was the Soviet ultimatum rather than American financial pressure that had saved Egypt. Khruschev himself was thus able to take the credit in the Middle East and the Communist World for having defeated the British and French 'imperialists'.

2 The Legacy of the Crises

> **KEY ISSUE** What were the consequences of the 1956 crises for Soviet and Western Blocs?

a) For the USSR

The Polish and Hungarian crises had showed how difficult it was for the Soviet government to encourage the satellite states to reform without creating a demand for their transformation into genuine democratic regimes. They also highlighted the problems the Soviet bloc had in the post Stalinist era in agreeing on common policies, as there was no framework for regular consultations. Khrushchev attempted to remedy this at the conference attended by the international Communist leaders at Moscow in October 1957. Although opposed by the Poles and the Yugoslavs, it passed a motion recognising the USSR as 'the first and mightiest' of the Socialist countries, while still acknowledging the legitimacy of the principle of 'different roads to Socialism'. It also made very clear that a Communist leader under pressure could appeal to the Soviet Bloc for 'mutual aid', which in effect meant military assistance to counter any major disturbances. An element of diversity was still tolerated and considerable economic help was given to the satellite states by the USSR, but it was understood that they must in all essentials stick to the Soviet political and economic model. Almost inevitably this doctrine led to a fresh break with Tito, who now joined with India and Egypt to form the 'Non Aligned Movement' of neutral states.

One of the important legacies of the Hungarian and Suez crises was that Khrushchev's position was greatly strengthened in the USSR. Dulles, the American Secretary of State, had perceptively warned that he was 'the most dangerous person to lead the Soviet Union since the October revolution'.[3] Unlike Stalin who attempted to calculate carefully the consequences of his actions, Dulles felt that he was prepared to take dangerous risks to achieve his ends.

After his propaganda success in the Suez Crisis Khrushchev was convinced that the mere threat of nuclear weapons would enable him to force the West to make concessions in Berlin and elsewhere. His policy of 'nuclear diplomacy' gained more credibility when the USSR launched the world's first intercontinental missile in August 1957, and followed it up by sending a satellite, the Sputnik, into orbit in October. Although the overall military balance still favoured the West, Khrushchev deliberately exaggerated the extent of the Soviet successes, in order, as he wrote in his memoirs, 'to exert pressure on American militarists – and also influence the minds of more reasonable politicians – so that the United States would start treating us better'.[4]

b) For NATO

The immediate damage done to NATO by the Suez crisis was quickly repaired, as was the Anglo-American special relationship; yet in Continental Western Europe as a whole, a certain distrust of American policies lingered. Once the Soviets were in a position to threaten the American East Coast cities with their new ICBM missiles, the European leaders wondered whether the Americans would still defend Western Europe from a possible Soviet attack. Rather than see New York and Washington destroyed would they not do a deal with the Soviets and surrender Western Europe or at least West Germany? These fears were strengthened by several current developments. The Americans and British were reducing their conventional forces in Europe and equipping those that remained with tactical nuclear weapons. In October 1957 Adam Rapacki, the Polish Foreign Minister, also put forward plans for a nuclear free zone in Central Europe, which Adenauer believed was a 'Russian trap' leading to the reunification of a neutralised Germany. Not surprisingly, therefore, Adenauer became more responsive to French plans in early 1958 for developing a Franco–German–Italian nuclear bomb independent of the British and Americans.

Doubts about America's loyalty to its European allies also influenced Adenauer's thinking about the future of the new European Economic Community, the EEC, and his attitude to General de Gaulle, who returned to power in France in May 1958. The two

A NOTE ON THE EEC AND EFTA

The EEC was set up by the Treaty of Rome, which was signed with general American approval by the FRG, France, Italy and the Benelux states in March 1957. Its aim was to create a common market or customs union within 12 years, whilst also gradually forming a more integrated political structure. British plans for setting up a much larger free trade zone were turned down by the leaders of the Six on the grounds that it would not provide an effective basis for European economic and political cooperation. This led to Britain forming the European Free Trade Association (EFTA) with Denmark, Norway, Sweden, Switzerland, Austria and Portugal. Thus a major economic split in Western Europe developed.

statesmen had very different plans for its future. Adenauer wanted it to develop into a closely integrated community linked to the USA, while the General hoped that it would become an association of independent states, completely free from American influence, and under French leadership. If, however, the Americans decided to pull out of Europe or sacrifice West Berlin to the USSR, de Gaulle's vision of Europe was the only alternative Adenauer could fall back on.

3 The Berlin Crisis, 1958–61

a) The First Stages of the Crisis

KEY ISSUE What was Khrushchev intending to achieve by triggering a crisis over Berlin?

In the Autumn of 1956 the GDR had acted as a 'clamp' which had helped to keep Poland and the East European satellite states from quitting the Soviet bloc. Yet the GDR, despite Soviet recognition in September 1955, remained a fragile and artificial state totally dependent on Moscow and the presence of 20 divisions of Russian troops stationed within its frontiers. It was confronted with a prosperous West Germany, the miraculous economic recovery of which inevitably attracted many of its youngest and most ambitious citizens. Through the open frontier in Berlin it was still possible to flee from the drab life of Socialist planning and rationing to the bright lights of the FRG, and both Adenauer and the USA did everything to encourage this. Between 1945 and 1961 altogether about one-sixth of the whole East German population had fled westwards. One way of stopping this exodus was dramatically to improve the standard of living in the GDR, but to achieve this, it was essential to stop skilled workers and professionals quitting in large numbers to the FRG. This meant that something had to be done about the status of West Berlin.

By the autumn of 1958 Khrushchev was increasingly confident that the USSR could force the USA into making concessions over West Berlin, and indeed perhaps over the whole German question. By grossly exaggerating the extent of Soviet nuclear power and by putting pressure on West Berlin he was sure that he could squeeze concessions from the Western Allies without the risk war of war. He graphically observed: 'Berlin is the testicles of the West ... every time I want to make the West scream I squeeze on Berlin'.[5] Also, as the Chinese pointed out, the whole prestige of international Communism was at stake, if the GDR could not be turned into a viable state able to hold its own with the FRG.

Apart from strengthening the GDR what other aims had Khrushchev in mind? He also hoped to:

- stop or at least delay the decision by NATO to equip the FRG with nuclear weapons;
- show his critics within the USSR and the Chinese that he was not 'soft on the imperialists';
- divide the Western Powers;
- force them to accept the USSR as a political and military equal and to come to the conference table to draw up a German peace treaty, which would recognise the division of Germany and the GDR's postwar frontiers with Poland.

In Hope Harrison's words 'Khrushchev always saw and used West Berlin ... as a lever to compel the West to recognize the post-war *status quo* and the existence of East Germany'.[6] The long and dangerous crisis began on 10 November when Khrushchev called for a peace treaty with the two German states:

ı Is it not time for us to draw appropriate conclusions from the fact that the key items of the Potsdam Agreement concerning the maintenance

of peace in Europe and, consequently, throughout the world, have been violated, and that certain forces continue to nurture German militarism,
5 prompting it in the direction in which it was pushed before the Second World War, that is, against the East? Is it not time for us to reconsider our attitude to this part of the Potsdam Agreement, and to denounce it? The time has obviously arrived for the signatories of the Potsdam Agreement to renounce the remnants of the occupation regime in
10 Berlin, and thereby make it possible to create a normal situation in the capital of the German Democratic Republic. The Soviet Union, for its part, would hand over to the sovereign German Democratic Republic the functions in Berlin that are still exercised by Soviet agencies. This, I think, would be the correct thing to do.

Nikita Khrushchev making a speech in an aggressive mood.

On 27 November he followed this up with a six month ultimatum demanding the demilitarisation of West Berlin, the withdrawal of Western troops, and its change of status into a 'free city'. If the Western Allies refused to sign a peace treaty with the two German states, Khrushchev threatened to conclude a peace agreement just with the GDR and to recognise its sovereignty over East Berlin. This would then enable it to control access to West Berlin and interfere at will with traffic using the land corridors from the FRG. The Western

Allies would thus be compelled to deal with East German rather than Russian officials and so in effect recognise the sovereignty of the GDR, which would shatter the Hallstein doctrine (see page 87). He was, however, as we shall see, to have second thoughts about putting quite so much power into Ulbricht's hands.

Although the Western Allies rejected the ultimatum, Khrushchev was successful in forcing them to the conference table to discuss 'the German question'. In February 1959 they agreed that a foreign ministers' conference should meet in Geneva in the summer. Khrushchev was also delighted to see splits beginning to appear in the Western alliance. In the preceding months Adenauer viewed with increasing alarm statements from London and Washington signalling the desire for compromise and concession, and inevitably drew closer to de Gaulle, who urged a much tougher line against the Soviets. He was particularly alarmed by Macmillan's decision to visit Moscow in February and by Eisenhower's invitation to Khrushchev to visit the USA in the coming autumn.

At the Geneva Conference both sides put forward proposals for German unity, but no agreement was secured. The Western Powers came up with their usual demand for free elections, while the USSR suggested that the two Germanies should form a confederation, which would only very slowly evolve into a united state. However, as the Soviets did succeed in persuading the West to discuss the Berlin problem as a separate issue, Khrushchev believed that his threats were paying off, and he continued the pressure, renewing the ultimatum in June.

Between 1959 and 1961 there were more summits that at any time since the Second World War. When Khrushchev visited Eisenhower at Camp David in September 1959, the mood was friendly, but, to quote Gaddis, the two leaders 'got no further than an agreement to diasagree'.[7] Over the next two years Khrushchev alternated periods of *détente*, when he temporarily allowed the ultimatum to lapse again, with spells of acute crisis during which further threats were devised, to force the West into making concessions over the status of Berlin and the future of Germany. His actions were not without success. Behind the scenes in London and Washington, and at times even in Paris, various schemes for creating a nuclear free zone in Central Europe, recognising Poland's Western frontiers and the GDR were considered quite seriously. Adenauer meanwhile was desperate to stop any of these plans from reducing the FRG to a neutral second rate state, but by May 1960 when the Paris Conference was due to open, he had no idea what Eisenhower and Macmillan might be about to propose. Thus for him at least it was 'a gift from heaven',[8] as Klessmann has called it, when Khrushchev used the shooting down of an American spy plane over Russia as an excuse to torpedo the summit, and wait until a new American President was elected in the Autumn.

U-2 SPY PLANES AND THE ARMS RACE

In 1956 the USA bought 53 Lockheed U-2 spy planes. Based in Japan, Turkey and Britain they were able to fly over Soviet territory and photo accurately military bases, missile factories and launch pads. By 1961 Soviet technology caught up with the U-2s, and on 5 May a Soviet anti-aircraft missile shot down a plane that had been sent to see whether there were missile bases in the Urals. These flights established that for all Khrushchev's boasting the Soviets possessed in the spring of 1961 very few ICBMs and no launching platforms for them. Indeed the USSR had only 4 ICBMs based on a site near Archangel.

b) The Construction of the Berlin Wall

KEY ISSUE Why was the Berlin Wall built and not immediately bulldozed down by the Western Allies?

Until the Autumn of 1960 Khrushchev determined the course of the Berlin crisis. Ulbricht, who certainly stood to benefit from a successful outcome, was little more than a spectator. Khrushchev still did not despair of using Berlin as a means to solve the German problem as a whole, and despite his bluster, he acted cautiously. He told Ulbricht in May 1960, for instance, that

> Under present conditions, it is worthwhile to wait a little longer and try to find a solution for the long-since ripe question of a peace treaty with the two German states. This will not escape our hands. We had better wait, and the matter will get more mature.

However, in desperation, as the numbers of refugees to the West dramatically increased during the years 1960–61, Ulbricht pressed Khrushchev to sign a separate peace treaty with the GDR, at one juncture sarcastically observing: 'You only *talk* about a peace treaty, but don't *do* anything about it'.[9] By this stage Ulbricht increasingly tried to use the very real threat of the collapse of the GDR to force Khrushchev to sign a separate peace treaty with it. Although the Soviet leader had indeed threatened the West with this, he was now reluctant to carry it out, because he feared that if the East Germans were given responsiblity for controlling the links between West Berlin and the FRG without the West's agreement, they might well provoke a major crisis, such as another blockade of West Berlin. Khrushchev was only using the *threat* of a separate peace to squeeze concessions from the West.

Khrushchev's hopes that John Kennedy, the new American

President, would make the concessions that Eisenhower had refused, proved unrealistic, but his response to Russian threats to West Berlin hinted at a possible solution to the Berlin problem. While he dramatically built up American forces in Europe, he also urged negotiation on the whole German question and pointedly stressed in a television broadcast on 25 July 1961 that the USA was essentially interested in free access to West Berlin rather than to Berlin as a whole. Kennedy was in fact indicating where the West would draw the line and fight if necessary. Up to this point Khrushchev had consistently rejected the option of closing off the East Berlin frontier. He had hoped rather to uncouple West Berlin from the FRG than to cut it off from East Germany. However, the growing unrest in the GDR caused by the forced collectivisation of agriculture and the ever increasing number of refugees to West Germany finally persuaded him that something had to be done to prevent an East German collapse. Somewhere between the end of July and the beginning of August Khrushchev decided that the East German border in Berlin would have to be closed. This decision was confirmed at a meeting of the Warsaw Pact states in Moscow on 3–5 August 1961, and in the early morning of 13 August the operation was efficiently and swiftly carried out. At first the border was sealed off with barbed wire, but when no Western countermeasures followed, a more permanent concrete wall was built.

The first Berlin crisis ended in complete failure for Stalin. Can it be argued that the second crisis was also a failure for Khrushchev? Like Stalin he had failed to force the Western Allies to withdraw their troops from West Berlin or to compel them to negotiate peace treaties with the two Germanies. On the other hand, with the construction of the Berlin Wall he had achieved a limited but important success for Soviet policies. By tolerating it the Western Powers in effect recognised East Germany. The Wall both consolidated the GDR, and ensured that the Soviet Union was still responsible for maintaining international access to West Berlin. In 1992 one former high ranking Soviet official explained to an American historian that:

1 the wall itself was the way with a lot of fuss and ceremony to bury the idea of a German peace treaty, in the sense of a separate treaty with the GDR. After the building of the Wall, the signing of a separate treaty with the GDR was not necessary. All issues that needed to be resolved
5 were resolved. Ulbricht saw in a peace treaty a way to receive international recognition. For us, international recognition was important, but not the most important. We saw this would happen no matter what; it was a question of time. After the borders were closed there would be no other choice than for the West to recognize the GDR.
10 And that is what happened.

4 Learning to Live with the Wall, 1961–63

> **KEY ISSUE** Why despite the construction of the Berlin Wall did tension remain high in Europe until 1963?

The prolonged crisis over Berlin effectively ended with the Wall, although this was not immediately obvious at the time. The Soviet Union renewed nuclear testing and on 30 October exploded an enormous bomb of over 50 megatons, which it was calculated could destroy an American state the size of Maryland. There was also continued tension along the Wall in Berlin. American troops were ostentatiously practising tearing down simulated walls, while on 27 October Soviet and American tanks stood almost muzzle to muzzle for several hours at Check Point Charlie, one of the few access points through the Wall. Khrushchev was determined to keep up the pressure on West Berlin. In October, for instance, he told the Soviet Foreign Minister, Gromyko, and the Polish leader, Gomulka, that 'we should . . . exploit the weakness of the enemy. We should strive to remove the official representatives from West Berlin'.[10]

In a series of talks with the Soviet leaders over the next year Kennedy attempted to lower the tension in Berlin by exploring the possibility of an agreement over Berlin, which would guarantee the rights of the Western Allies, whilst recognising what he called the 'legitimate interests of others'. By this, of course, he meant the USSR and GDR. Inevitably Adenauer regarded these negotiations with great suspicion and dreaded that Kennedy would end up sacrificing West Berlin. Consequently he drew even closer to Gaullist France, signing in January 1963 the Franco-German Treaty of Friendship and supporting the French veto on Britain's application to join the EEC (see page 114).

In October 1962 the Cuban crisis temporarily forced the Berlin question into second place and rallied the Western powers around Kennedy. After the crisis, discussions on Berlin continued, but the

THE CUBAN CRISIS

The Cuban crisis was a direct confrontaion between the USA and the USSR, involving neither NATO nor the Warsaw Pact. Khrushchev began secretly in the Summer of 1962 to deploy nuclear missiles on Cuba backed up by 40,000 Soviet troops. The point of this highly dangerous manoeuvre was to gain a base from which the US could be threatened by medium range Soviet missiles. This would correct the strategic imbalance caused by the construction of American missiles bases in Turkey and Western Europe. He also wanted to defend the Communist leader of the Cuban revolution, Fidel Castro, from a possible American attack. Castro had seized power in 1959 and come into increasing conflict with the Americans. On 14 October an American U-2 spy plane discovered the missiles. Until Khrushchev agreed on 27 October to remove them in return for an American guarantee not to invade Cuba and secret assurances that it would dismantle the 15 Jupiter missiles in Turkey, there developed the most dangerous crisis of the whole Cold War.

need to find a settlement was no longer so urgent. Having come so close to nuclear war in Cuba, Khrushchev shied away from another confrontation in Berlin and accepted that for the time being the Wall had consolidated the GDR. The Soviet government also began to reassess its policies and priorities in light of the lessons learnt in the Cuban missile crisis. As far as they affected Europe these will be analysed in Chapter 7.

5 Assessment: The 'Second Cold War'

> **KEY ISSUE** How accurate is it to describe the whole period 1956–63 as the 'Second Cold War'?

In 1955 it seemed that the Cold War in Europe, if not over, had at least stabilised. The Soviets had pulled out of Austria (see page 87) and there was much talk about the Geneva spirit. Yet over the next six years little progress was made towards *détente*, as relations between the Warsaw Pact states and the North Atlantic Alliance deteriorated to level not seen since the Berlin Blockade of 1948/9. Do the reasons for this lie with Khrushchev or were there deeper causes?

A major cause of European instability was the failure of the USSR to set up in Eastern Europe what the Americans managed to create in Western Europe: 'an empire by invitation' (see page 67). The Destalinisation policies of 1953–56 were attempts to create more popular regimes that did not depend on terror and the Red Army to survive, and to allow the peoples of Eastern Europe some input into influencing their own politics. Yet the Polish riots and the Hungarian revolt of 1956 showed how hard it was to get the balance between liberalisation and the maintenance of essential control. This was to remain one of the main dilemmas facing the Soviet leadership for the next 33 years.

Until 1961 the division of Germany and the unsolved problem of Berlin also remained a major destabilising factor in Europe. The root of the problem was the chronic economic weakness of East Germany, which could only be remedied by closing the inner Berlin frontier. This, however, would violate the Potsdam agreement and cause a major crisis involving the USA and its allies. Both German states depended for their existence on their Superpower protector. As neither the USA nor the USSR could allow their part of Germany to collapse or be absorbed by the rival bloc, the two German leaders, Ulbricht and Adenauer, had at times immense influence over the foreign policy of Moscow and Washington respectively. Thus Adenauer did much to stop Eisenhower from effectively exploring the possibilities of a Berlin settlement in the period 1958–60, while recent research by Hope Harrison has shown that it was finally pressure from Ulbricht that propelled Khrushchev into building the Berlin Wall.

The crises of 1956 and 1958–61 were triggered by instabilities within the Soviet Bloc and Central Europe, but they were made far more dangerous by Khrushchev's high risk 'nuclear diplomacy'. In 1956 by threatening to bombard Britain, France and Israel with nuclear missiles, even when in reality the USSR had not yet developed the military capacity to do this, he was able to pose as the saviour of Egypt. He did not hesitate to use the ultimate threat of nuclear weapons as a bargaining counter in both the Berlin and Cuba crises. Yet, as we have seen, much of this was only 'bluff and bluster'.[11] In that sense Khrushchev very much presided over a period of acute tension which perhaps could be called a 'Second Cold War'. In other ways the Khrushchev years set the pattern for the next three decades in Europe. The Berlin Wall, however cruel, did at last stabilise the GDR and with it Central Europe. It also enabled both Superpowers, as Gaddis has put it, to 'break loose' from their German allies and explore the possibility of *détente* in Europe.[12] Paradoxically Khrushchev was also the father of *détente*. Despite his brinkmanship over Berlin and Cuba he aimed for peaceful economic and ideological competition with the West. After the Cuban Crisis Soviet policy settled down, as we shall see in the next chapter, to a dual policy of achieving *détente* in Europe and nuclear equality with the USA.

References

1 G. Roberts, *The Soviet Union in World Politics* (Routledge, 1999), p. 41.
2 'Hungary and Poland, 1956: Khrushchev's CPSU CC Presidium Meeting on East European Crises, 24 October 1956', introduction, translation and annotation by Mark Kramer, *Cold War International History Project Bulletin (CWIHP)* (Woodrow Wilson International Center for Scholars, Washington, DC.) on the Internet at cwihp.si.edu, p. 9.
3 J.L. Gaddis, *We Now Know* (OUP, 1997), p. 239.
4 *Ibid.,* p. 239.
5 *Ibid.,* p. 140.
6 H. Harrison, 'Ulbricht and the Concrete Rose: New Archival Evidence on the Dynamics of Soviet-East German Relations and the Berlin Crisis, 1958–61', *Cold War International History Project (CWIHP)* at cwihp.si.edu, p. 7.
7 Gaddis, *op.cit.,* p. 142.

8 C. Klessmann, quoted in D.G. Williamson, *Germany From Defeat to Partition, 1945–63* (Pearson, 2001), p. 89.
9 Gaddis, *op.cit.*, p. 144.
10 'Rough Notes from a Conversation (Gromyko, Khrushchev and Gomulka on the International Situation, n.d. [October 1961]', *Cold War International History Project Bulletin (CWIHP)* on the Internet at cwihp.si.edu, pp. 2–3.
11 Roberts, *op.cit.*, p. 59.
12 Gaddis, *op.cit.*, p. 150.

Summary Diagram
Khrushchev and the 'Second Cold War'

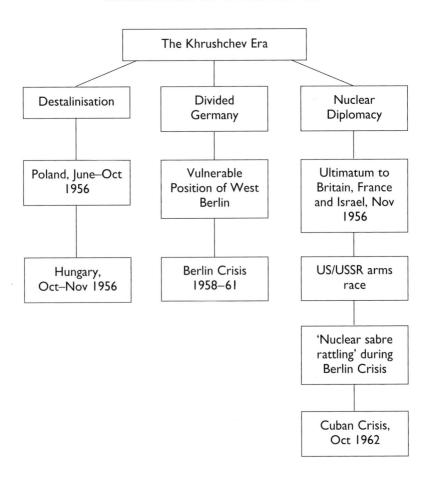

Working on Chapter 6

This chapter covers one of the most important periods of the Cold War in Europe. In making notes on it you must make sure that you understand what Khrushchev was hoping to accomplish. First of all show what destalinisation was, and how and why it caused major crises in Poland and Hungary in 1956. Then look at Khrushchev's response to these two crises and note how it varied. It is particularly important to grasp how, in Khrushchev's mind, the Hungarian crisis was linked with the Suez crisis. Finally make a list of what the consequences of the upheavals of 1956 for both blocs were.

The causes and course of the Berlin Crisis of 1958–61 are an important part of this chapter. In making notes on them make clear how Khrushchev tried to use the status of West Berlin as a lever to force concessions on the German problem as a whole from the West. Only gradually, under considerable pressure from Ulbricht, did he agree to the minimum option of the Wall. What was the Western reaction to this? Why did it tolerate the Wall and in what ways can it be said that the Wall stabilised the situation in Germany and perhaps in Europe as a whole?

Answering structured and essay questions on Chapter 6

The years 1956 and 1958–61 are of pivotal importance in the Cold War and are ideal topics for structured questions to focus on. Typical examples of such questions are:

I. a) Outline the causes of unrest in the Soviet bloc in 1956.
   b) Explain why Soviet troops intervened in Hungary, but not Poland.
   c) Did the Berlin Crisis of 1958–61 end in a success for the USSR?

Question a) is essentially testing you on your knowledge of the facts. You need to give careful thought to what is relevant here and get the balance between longer term or background causes and the immediate causes. The 'Geneva spirit' (see page 87), destalinisation, the improvement in Soviet–Yugoslav relations and to a lesser extent Western propaganda broadcasing form the context in which the unrest broke out. Then you will need to look at short term causes, such at the Poznan riots, the consequences of the release of Gomulka from prison and the dismissal of Rákosi in Hungary. Question b) is more complex. You must not just give an account of Soviet policy towards Poland and Hungary in October–November 1956, but also show *why* it differed. Khrushchev was wary of the danger of Soviet troops becoming trapped in a bitter struggle in Poland, and Gomulka, after all, was a Communist, who was committed to restoring order. In Hungary by 30 October there was a real danger that

Communism would collapse. Nagy was not only wanting to leave the Warsaw Pact, but also to turn the clock back to 1946/47 and allow non-Communist parties to re-enter government. Both Tito and Khrushchev feared the 'domino effect' of this on the other Eastern bloc states. Question c) again requires you to make a judgement. On the one hand Khrushchev failed to dislodge the Western Powers from West Berlin and persuade them to sign peace treaties with both Germanies. On the other hand the Wall did consolidate the GDR and stop it from collapsing. Eventually it also ensured that in time the Western Allies and the FRG would have to recognise the GDR.

The following are essay questions which require a wider range of knowledge and more extensive answers:

1. If Khruschchev was really aiming at peaceful competition with the Western Powers and liberalisation in Eastern Europe, why was his European policy often so aggressive?
2. Why did the crises of 1956 and 1958–61 not lead to war?

These are more wide-ranging essay questions, which require a considerable amount of planning before you write them out. In the introduction formulate clearly and briefly your main arguments and then develop each of them in separate paragraphs in the rest of your essay. In question 1 you should first of all show what Khrushchev understood by peaceful competition: he did not want war but believed that the Soviet Bloc would eventually overtake the West and also attract overwhelming support from the Third World. He was, however, often impulsive and opportunist and would take risks to strengthen the USSR's bargaining position. You will need to explain how he used 'nuclear diplomacy' to frighten the Western Powers and to try to squeeze concessions from them. The main part of the essay will be an analysis of the crises of destalinisation in 1956 and the Berlin crisis of 1958–61, which is essentially what the question means by 'aggressive policies'. You will also need to explain how Khrushchev's attempt to destalinise, win back Tito and reform the structure of control within the Soviet bloc led first to the Poznan riots and then to the Hungarian revolt, which he had little option but to crush. In the much more complicated Berlin Crisis his aims were also to a certain extent defensive, but they were dangerously open-ended and pursued in a way which created great tension. He wished to use the status of West Berlin as a lever to gain major concessions from Western Powers, which would go far to solving the German problem in the interests of the USSR. In the end he achieved little apart from building the Berlin Wall. In your conclusion you could, however, stress that this was a defensive action that stopped the GDR from collapsing.

The next question again refers to the two great crises of the Khrushchev period. It is simply put, but you need to plan your answer carefully before writing it out. Firstly you need to show that the Western Powers had no intention of intervening to help the

Hungarians in 1956. It is true that the Suez crisis complicated the issue, but Eisenhower was particularly careful not to provoke the Soviets over an issue that might lead to war. He accepted that Hungary and Poland were in the Soviet sphere of influence. Similarly Britain and the USA had no desire to pull down the Berlin wall in 1961, and were anxious to negotiate a settlement that would preserve the rights of the Western Allies while recognising Soviet and GDR interests. Secondly you must again explore how much of Khrushchev's 'nuclear diplomacy' was in fact based on bluff.

Source-based questions on Chapter 6

1 The Impact of Destalinization
Study the extracts on pages 94, 95 and 96.

a) Read the communiqué on page 94.
What policy towards the satellite states does it suggest that the Soviet government will adopt? (*3 marks*)

b) Read the extract from the Soviet Central Committee meeting of 24 October 1956 on page 95.
What does Gomulka mean by 'they would not permit their independence to be taken away' (lines 2–3)? Using your own knowledge and this document explain why Khrushchev accepted this. (*5 marks*)

c) Read the extract on page 96.
What reasons is Khrushchev putting forward to justify soviet intervention in Hungary? (*5 marks*)

d) Do the extracts on pages 95 and 96 explain why the policy laid down in the communiqué of 20 June (page 94) was difficult to carry out? (*7 marks*)

2 The Berlin Crisis, 1958–61
Study the extracts on pages 100–01, 103 and 104.

a) Read the extracts on pages 100–01.
What does Khrushchev mean by 'key items of the Potsdam Agreement ... have been violated' (lines 2–4). Explain your answer fully. (*5 marks*)

b) Read the extracts on pages 103 and 104 and use your knowledge.
Do these extracts indicate that Khrushchev's aims during the Berlin crisis were really to consolidate the GDR? (*10 marks*)

7 The 'Long Peace' in Europe?: *Détente*, the 'New Cold War' and the Collapse of the Soviet Bloc, 1964–91

POINTS TO CONSIDER

The first part of the chapter looks at the causes of *détente* and shows how it meant different things for not only the USSR and the USA but also the European powers, particularly the FRG, which developed its own *Ostpolitik* (policy towards Eastern Europe). It then focuses on the treaties of 1970–73, which regulated the FRG's relations with the USSR, the GDR, Poland and Czechoslovakia, and on the negotiations which led to the successful conference in Helsinki on 'Security and Cooperation in Europe'. You will see that these agreements did much to lessen tension in Europe, although they failed to prevent the outbreak of a 'New Cold War' in 1979. Finally, as you read the concluding section of the chapter, ask yourself why the Cold War in Europe ended as it did. Was the collapse of the Soviet Bloc really so unexpected?

KEY DATES

1963	5 Aug	Test Ban Treaty.
1964	15 Oct	Fall of Khrushchev.
1965	7 Feb	US bombing of North Vietnam starts.
1966	Mar	France withdraws from NATO.
1967	Dec	Harmel report on NATO.
1968	21–27 Aug	Invasion of Czechoslovakia.
1969	28 Sept	Willy Brandt elected.
	17 Nov	SALT talks begin.
1970	12 Aug	USSR–FRG Treaty.
	7 Dec	Warsaw Treaty.
1971	3 Sept	Four Power Treaty on Berlin.
1972	21 Dec	Basic Treaty between FRG and GDR.
1973	1 Jan	Britain joins EC.
1975	1 Aug	Helsinki Final Act.
1979	27 Dec	Soviet invasion of Afghanistan.
1980	13 Dec	Martial law declared in Poland.
1982	Nov	Brezhnev succeeded by Andropov.
1983	Nov	FRG accepts new medium range missiles.
1985	12 Mar	Gorbachev becomes USSR Party Leader.
	1 Nov	Reagan–Gorbachev summit at Geneva.

1986	**2 Oct**	Summit at Reykjavik.
1989	**June**	Elections in Poland.
	Sept	Hungary allows GDR citizens through frontier to Austria.
	9 Nov	Berlin Wall breached.
1990	**3 Oct**	Germany reunified.
1991	**26 Dec**	USSR formally dissolved.

1 The Road to *Détente*, 1963–69

> **KEY ISSUES** How much progress was made towards *détente* in Europe in 1963–69 and what problems had to be overcome?

After the Cuban missile crisis the nature of the Cold War in Europe changed. A new period of stability emerged, which has sometimes been called 'the long peace'. Both the two Superpowers and the Western European states sought *détente* in Europe, although they all interpreted the meaning of *détente* differently. The Americans were heavily involved in the Vietnam war, and wanted *détente* to stabilise Europe and restrain the USSR, while the USSR was also facing a growing challenge from China. Consequently it hoped that *détente* would lead Washington and its Allies permanently to accept the postwar

THE DISTRACTED SUPERPOWERS

Sino-Soviet relations had been deteriorating since the late 1950s. The Chinese were highly critical of Khrushchev's belief in peaceful competition between the USA and USSR and scornful of his apparent failure in Cuba. Fearing that China might risk a nuclear war against the USA, which would also involve the USSR, Khrushchev had refused to carry out his promises of supplying China with nuclear weapons. Throughout the 1960s Soviet–Chinese relations rapidly grew worse. In 1966 the Soviet and Chinese Communist Parties severed all fraternal links, and the USSR even began to target some of its missiles on China. In 1969 there were large scale border clashes along the Sino-Soviet frontier.

At the same time the USA became ever more deeply involved in Vietnam. To stop the Communists in the North from taking over South Vietnam the Americans committed an increasing number of 'military advisers' or troops. In 1966 there were 400,000 US troops in Vietnam. By 1968 it had become clear that the Americans were losing the war, but it was not until 1973 that the last soldiers finally left and President Nixon was able to negotiate a cease-fire. In 1975 the Communists took over South Vietnam.

division of Europe, and to agree to something approaching nuclear parity between the USA and USSR. For the French *détente* was a way of undermining the influence of both Superpowers in Europe so that the individual European states could regain their freedom, while for the West Germans it was an essential precondition for remaining in contact with and helping their fellow citizens in the GDR.

a) Developments in Western Europe, 1964–68

The Test Ban treaty of 1963, signed by Britain, the USSR and the USA, banning nuclear tests in the atmosphere, under water and in outer space, and the Nuclear non-Proliferation Treaty in 1968 were the most significant achievements in the early period of *détente*. These agreements were welcome in Western Europe, but essentially they assumed a world divided into two blocs led by their respective super-power. By 1968, however, the Vietnam war was causing a rising wave of anti-Americanism. America was both failing to win the war and, as a result of its ruthless but ineffective military tactics, losing its position as the moral leader of the West. Its European allies rejected President Johnston's argument that the war was a vital part of the global confrontation with Communism, and instead concentrated on easing tensions within Europe. This task was made easier by the fall of Khrushchev in October 1964 and his replacement by Brezhnev and Kosygin. Brezhnev, who rapidly emerged as the key figure in the USSR, was less erratic than Khrushchev and appeared to be more of a conciliator and consensus seeker, with whom the West European leaders thought they could negotiate.

Potentially the disagreements over the Vietnam war and the increasing assertiveness of the West European states could have destroyed NATO and led to an American withdrawal from Western Europe. De Gaulle took the lead in the attack on American influence in Western Europe. In 1963 he vetoed Britain's application to join the EEC, on the grounds that Britain's was still too pro-Amercan, and three years later he both withdrew French forces from NATO and expelled its headquarters from Paris. He followed this up with a visit to the USSR, where he announced that the European states should liberate themselves from the 'bloc-mentality' of the Cold War. He also did all he could to weaken the dollar at a time when the US was beginning to come under financial pressure as a result of the costs of the Vietnam war. The West Germans were meanwhile cautiously beginning to put out feelers to Eastern Europe by setting up Trade missions in Yugoslavia and Romania. *Ostpolitik* took on a more definite shape when the Social Democrat leader, Willy Brandt, became Foreign Minister in December 1966. The key to his policy was that German unification was a long term goal that could only gradually be reached within the context of a European *détente*.

Given the prosperity of Western Europe, its refusal to assist the

Americans in Vietnam and the determination of its leading states to pursue their own ways to *détente*, it was not surprising that in 1967 the American Senator, Michael Mansfield, put forward a motion in Congress urging the withdrawal of the majority of US troops from Europe, which was only defeated by 49 votes. Both to persuade Congress to continue to support the US military involvement in Europe and to prevent his allies from following the French example and leaving NATO, President Johnson committed himself to negotiate mutual and balanced force reductions with Moscow, although negotiations did not start until 1972. In December 1967 a high powered NATO committee chaired by the Belgian Foreign Minister, Pierre Hamel, drew up a report which committed NATO not only to defending Western Europe, but also to reaching a *détente* with the Warsaw Pact states. It stressed that:

> 1 Collective defence is a stabilising factor in world politics. It is the necessary condition for effective policies directed towards a greater relaxation of tensions. The way to peace and stability in Europe rests in particular on the use of the Alliance constructively in the interests of
> 5 *détente*. The participation of the USSR and USA will be necessary to achieve a settlement of the political problems in Europe.

The Hamel Report redefined NATO's role in the age of *détente* and prevented the political fall-out from the Vietnam War destroying the Western Alliance.

b) Divisions Within the Warsaw Pact

The Soviet retreat from Cuba, the growing atmosphere of *détente* and the Sino-Soviet split all combined to weaken Soviet control over Eastern Europe and provide some opportunities for the satellite states to pursue their own policies. Poland, for instance, wished to expand her trade with the West, while Romania was interested in normalising relations with the FRG. In an attempt to stop these independent initiatives the Warsaw Pact issued in 1966 the Bucharest Declaration, which tried to define what the whole Soviet bloc wanted to achieve through *détente*. This called for:

- the recognition of postwar frontiers in Eastern Europe;
- the creation of a new European security system;
- a veto on nuclear weapons for West Germany;
- a programme for economic, scientific and technical cooperation between East and West.

The Soviet Government's efforts to consolidate its control over Eastern Europe and to coordinate the foreign and military policies of the Warsaw Pact suffered a serious setback when in January 1968 Alexander Dubcek became the First Secretary of the Czech Communist Party. Like Nagy in Hungary in 1956 (see page 96), he attempted to create a socialist system that would be based on the consent of the people. In April 1968 he unveiled his programme for democratic change and modernisation of the economy, which marked the start of what was called the Prague Spring. In June he actually abolished censorship, which led to a flood of anti-Soviet propaganda being published in Czechosloavakia. Inevitably these developments began to worry Brezhnev and the other leaders of the Warsaw Pact, who after meeting on 15 July warned Dubcek that:

1 We cannot reconcile ourselves ... with the fact of hostile forces pushing your country off the road of Socialism and creating a threat of tearing away Czechoslovakia from the Socialist community. This is NO longer only your concern. This is the common concern of all commu-
5 nists and workers' parties and of states united by alliance co-operation and friendship....

THE ECONOMIC CONSEQUENCES OF THE BREZHNEV DOCTRINE

With the fall of Dubcek and the announcement of the Brezhnev doctrine, economic experiments aimed at modernisation and increased competitiveness in the Soviet bloc were discouraged and gradually halted. There was, instead, a return to the Stalinist style of centralised control of the economy with its emphasis on heavy industry. For a time this did appear to work. *Détente* and *Ostpolitik* opened the way up for generous Western loans to the USSR and the satellite states, which helped keep energy prices down and pay for massive industrial projects. However by the early 1980s the Eastern bloc economies were falling far behind the West. The total production of the USSR, for instance, was only 37 per cent of the Gross National Product of the USA. The Western European economies had been badly hit by the escalating rises in oil prices, which started in 1973, but they had responded to this challenge by modernising their economies and developing new industries and technologies such as computers. The USSR and its satellite states had failed to do this. They were therefore very vulnerable when faced with the triple crisis of inflation, rising oil prices and global economic depression in the early 1980s. Soviet economic growth collapsed, just at the time when the USSR was trapped in a large scale war in Afghanistan (see page 123) and the interest rates on American and West Germans loans were significantly increased. This was the economic scenario that confronted Gorbachev when he came to power in 1985 and led to the collapse of Communism (see pages 124–28).

Although Dubcek reluctantly agreed to restore censorship, Brezhnev had no confidence that he would succeed, and during the night of 20–1 August 20 divisions of Warsaw Pact troops provided by the USSR, Hungary, Poland, the GDR and Bulgaria invaded Czechoslovakia and terminated the 'Prague Spring'. In November Brezhnev defended the invasion by again stressing that any threat to Socialism in a Warsaw Pact country was also a threat to its allies. To counter this, collective intervention, as happened in Czechslovakia, would be justified. This became known as the Brezhnev doctrine and was only abandoned by Gorbachev in 1989 (see page 125).

The invasion of Czechoslovakia was, as Michel Debré, the French Prime Minister put it, 'a traffic accident on the road to *détente'*. It slowed down but did not halt progress. The election of Richard Nixon to the American Presidency in November 1968 and of Willy Brandt to the West German Chancellorship in October 1969 with a mandate for his *Ostpolitik* policy was soon to give it fresh impetus.

2 *Ostpolitik*

> **KEY ISSUES** What were the aims of Brandt's *Ostpolitik* and how did he seek to achieve them?

Brandt negotiated a complex set of inter-locking treaties which marked a major turning point in the Cold War. On one level Brandt's policy was primarily a matter of coming to terms with the postwar world. This, of course, involved the recognition of the East German regime, although his whole strategy, by defusing the tense situation between the two Germanies, was also aimed at leaving the door ajar for future unification. *Ostpolitik* was not conducted in a vacuum. Brandt had gained the support of the USA and his NATO allies by emphasising that the FRG did not intend to quit NATO or the EC. In the course of 1970–2 five sets of intricate and inter-dependent agreements were negotiated: the treaties between the FRG, USSR, Poland, Czechoslovakia and the GDR and then the Four Power Agreement on Berlin.

a) The Moscow, Warsaw and Prague Treaties, 1970–3

No progress could be made in *Ostpolitik* until relations between the FRG and the USSR were improved. The FRG's signature of the Nuclear Non-Proliferation Treaty in 1969, its readiness to increase technological and economic links with the USSR and willingness to agree to a European security conference, which Moscow hoped would confirm its postwar control over Eastern Europe, were all preliminary concessions that helped pave the way to a treaty with Moscow. After prolonged and difficult negotiations the 'foundation stone of

Ostpolitik',[1] as A.J. Nicholls calls the Moscow Treaty, was eventually signed on 12 August by Brandt and Brezhnev. In this the USSR and FRG declared that they had no territorial claims against any other state. The FRG recognised both the 'non-violability' of Poland's western frontier and of the inner German frontier. In a second part of the treaty the FRG committed itself to negotiating treaties with Poland, the GDR and Czechoslovakia. While the FRG still did not officially recognise the GDR, it agreed to abandon the Hallstein doctrine (see page 87) and accept that both Germanies would eventually become members of the United Nations. The Russians had in effect gained West German recognition of their European empire, yet this recognition was not unconditional. The West Germans also presented Brezhnev with a 'letter on German unity'. This stressed the FRG's right to work towards a state of peace in Europe in which 'the German people regains its unity in free self determination'.[2] Similarly the term 'inviolable' (not to be attacked or violated) as applied to the Oder-Neisse line and the inner-German frontier, rather than the preferred Soviet word 'immutable'(unchangeable), arguably kept the door open for a later peaceful revision of the frontier. Finally the ratification of the treaty was made dependent on a four power agreement over Berlin.

Negotiations with the Poles ran parallel with the Moscow talks and were completed in December 1970. Both states recognised that they had no territorial demands on each other and that the Oder-Neisse line was 'inviolable'. Trade and financial assistance from the FRG was to be increased, while the ethnic Germans still within Poland were to be allowed to emigrate to West Germany. In June 1973 a similar agreement was signed with Czechoslovakia, which specifically made the Munich Treaty of 1938 'void'.

b) Four Power Negotiations over Berlin

In March 1970, Four Power discussions began on the thorny problem of access to West Berlin. The involvement of Britain, France and the USA in these negotiations sent signals to both NATO and the Warsaw pact that *Ostpolitik* would not lead to a weakening of the FRG's links with the West. The Western Allies wanted a settlement underwritten by the USSR, which would finally confirm West Berlin's links with the FRG and guarantee its freedom of access to the West. At first the Russians were anxious to avoid making too many concessions, but their desire both for a general European security conference and reluctance to annoy President Nixon at a time when he was planning to improve relations with China made them more responsive to Western demands. The agreement, signed on 3 September 1971, was a 'milestone in the history of divided Berlin and divided Germany'.[3] The Soviets conceded three vital principles:

- unimpeded traffic between West Berlin and the FRG;

- recognition of West Berlin's ties with the FRG;
- and finally the right for West Berliners to visit East Berlin.

In return Britain, France and the USA agreed that the Western sectors of Berlin were not legally part of the FRG, even if in practice they had been so ever since West Berlin adopted the FRG's constitution in 1950.

The Berlin Wall in the 1970s.

c) The Basic Treaty

Once the Moscow Treaty and the agreement on Berlin had been signed, the way was open for direct negotiations between the GDR and FRG. For the GDR an agreement with the FRG was not without risk. If successful, it would undoubtedly secure the GDR international recognition, but at the continued risk of closer contact with the magnetic social and economic forces of the West. In July Brezhnev stressed to the somewhat sceptical Honecker, who had just replaced Ulbricht as the GDR leader, the solid advantages of the treaty for the GDR in that '[i]ts frontiers, its existence will be confirmed for all the world to see ...'. However, he also warned him that Brandt was aiming ultimately at the 'Social Democratisation' (converting the Communist SED into a more moderate Western style Social democratic party) of the GDR, and added: 'It ... must not come to a process of rapprochement [establishing close relations] between the FRG and the

GDR ... Concentrate everything on the all-sided strengthening of the GDR, as you call it'.[4]

First of all a series of technical agreements on transit traffic, the rights of West Berliners to visit East Berlin, and on postal communications were concluded. Then the two states moved on to negotiate the more crucial Basic Treaty, which was signed in December 1972. In it the FRG recognised the GDR as an equal and sovereign state and also accepted that both states should be represented at the United Nations. The FRG did, however, stress that it still considered the people of the GDR to have a common German citizenship and in a 'Letter Concerning German Unity', which it presented to East Berlin, it repeated its determination to work peacefully for German reunification.

The existence of the two Germanies now seemed to be a permanent fact confirmed by treaty. The two German states joined the United Nations in 1973. Within their respective blocs both the FRG and the GDR played increasingly important economic, military and political roles. Nothing, however, had changed the essential vulnerability of the GDR, whose very existence in the last resort still depended on Russian bayonets, as the events of 1989–90 were to show (see pages 126–7).

3 The Helsinki Accord

> **KEY ISSUES** What were the terms of the Helsinki Accord? Did the East or West benefit more from them?

In July 1973 the conference on security and co-operation opened in Helsinki. Robert Hutchings has called it the 'centrepiece of Soviet and East European diplomacy' in the 1970s.[5] Essentially the USSR wanted to persuade the West to recognise as permanent the territorial and political division of Europe made at Yalta (see pages 28–9), whilst stepping up economic, scientific and technological cooperation. It was anxious to exploit Western know-how and technology to modernise its economy. The USA initially consented to holding the Conference in return for a Soviet agreement on Berlin and the opening of negotiations at Vienna on mutual reductions of troops and armaments in Central Europe. It also used the Conference as a means to extract from the USSR concessions on human rights, which in time could bring about fundamental changes in the Soviet Bloc and lead to a loosening of Soviet control over the satellites. The subsequent Helsinki Agreement marked the high point of *détente* and was signed on 1 August 1975 by 33 European states, Canada and the USA. It was divided into three sections or 'baskets' as they were called:

- The first dealt with 'Questions relating to Security in Europe' and laid down a set of principles, which were to guide the participating states in their relations with each other. These included peaceful settlement of disputes, non-interference in internal affairs of other states and the 'inviolability' of frontiers. Brezhnev had hoped initially that he would be able to negotiate a peace treaty permanently guaranteeing the new postwar frontiers, but under West German pressure, Henry Kissinger, the American Secretary of State, managed to persuade the Soviets to accept the eventual possibility of a 'peaceful change to frontiers'.

- 'Basket two' concerned cooperation in 'the field of economics, of science and technology and the environment'.
- 'Basket Three' called for 'cooperation in humanitarian and other fields'. This meant expanding trade, tourism and cultural contacts between the two blocs, as well as promoting the reunion of families split up by the Iron Curtain.
- Finally there was to be a follow up conference two years later to work out further measures for European security and cooperation.

Who gained most from Helsinki? At first glance perhaps it could be argued that Brezhnev had achieved Western recognition of the Soviet Empire and an end to all attempts to undermine it. Right-wing politicians, like Margaret Thatcher in Britain and Ronald Reagan in the US, saw it, to quote the latter, as a 'new Yalta' placing 'the American seal of approval on the Soviet Empire in Eastern Europe'.[6] While there was some truth in this, Helsinki's stress on human rights and fundamental freedoms, as well as the increased East–West contact it encouraged, did in the medium term contain the potential for undermining the unpopular Soviet dominated regimes in Eastern Europe. Martin Walker has called the Helsinki Treaties 'a time bomb planted in the heart of the Soviet Empire'.[7]

4 The 'New Cold War', 1979–85

> **KEY ISSUE** How justified are historians in referring to the period 1979–85 as the 'New Cold War'?

a) The Weakening of Détente

International developments over the next decade were to confirm Nixon's comment that '*détente* does not mean the end of danger … *détente* is not the same as lasting peace'.[8] The USSR intensified its efforts to intervene and support sympathetic regimes in the Middle East, Africa and Asia, while the new American President, Jimmy Carter, partly to deflect criticism of the Helsinki Treaty, made human rights in Eastern Europe one of the priorities of his foreign policy.

The first major blow to the new Helsinki spirit came when Moscow

THE SOLIDARITY CRISIS IN POLAND, 1980–82

In 1980 strikes broke out in the shipyards in Gdansk over the question of price increases. The Government made far reaching economic and political concessions, and in August recognised the *Solidarity* movement as an independent trade union. At first it tried to claim that this concession only applied to Gdansk, but this provoked a wave of labour unrest culminating in the threat of a national strike. Both Brezhnev and the other Warsaw Pact leaders urged the Polish Prime Minister, Stanislaw Kania, to crush the 'anti-Socialist opposition forces'. Honecker wanted Brezhnev to send in troops. In a letter dated 28 November 1980 he wrote:

> According to information we have received through various channels, counterrevolutionary forces in the People's Republic of Poland are on constant offensive, any delay in acting against them would mean death – the death of socialist Poland.

Warsaw Pact forces were mobilised in early December, but at the last moment intervention was cancelled as Kania convinced Brezhnev that he could restore order himself. American warnings against the use of force were probably also a powerful deterrent. In 1981 *Solidarity* began to call for further drastic political changes. Once more the question of Soviet intervention arose, but eventually Moscow agreed in December to a declaration of Martial Law by General Jaruzelski, Kania' successor. The Americans had again called on the USSR to allow the Poles to solve the crisis themselves. Arguably this indicated to Jaruzelski that Washington would tolerate the declaration of martial law provided Soviet troops did not cross the frontier.

placed in 1976 SS-20 medium range missiles in Eastern Europe. This led to NATO adopting in 1979 the controversial two-track policy, whereby the US would deploy its own medium range Pershing and Cruise missiles in Western Europe by 1983 if no agreement could first be reached with the USSR. Both the Soviet invasion of Afghanistan in December 1979, which aimed at stabilising the situation there and restoring a regime friendly to the USSR, and the declaration of martial law (temporary military rule) in Poland in December 1981 further weakened *détente* and led to what historians now describe as the 'New Cold War'.

Although the prolonged struggle in Poland over *Solidarity* did have the potential for causing a major international incident, the 'New Cold War' never produced situations on the scale of the Berlin crises of 1948–9 and 1958–61. In face of the threat posed by the Soviet

SS-20s the Western Alliance also worked together more harmoniously. Margaret Thatcher and Ronald Reagan, who was elected American President in 1980, re-established at least the semblance of the old Anglo-American special relationship, while under President Mitterand the French cooperated much more closely with NATO, and in 1983, despite mounting public protest from the Greens and the left-wing of the SPD, Chancellor Helmut Kohl deployed the Pershing and Cruise missiles in West Germany.

b) *Ostpolitik* Under Threat

Ostpolitik, which was a product of *détente*, was inevitably threatened by the 'New Cold War'. Both Chancellor Helmut Schmidt (1974–83), who had played a leading role in alerting the Western Alliance to the dangers of the SS-20s, and his successor, Kohl, tried to protect it from the consequences of the sharply deterioriating East–West relations. At Tito's funeral in Belgrade in May 1980 Schmidt observed to Honecker that the European states must ensure that 'the really big brothers don't get nervous'.[9] A month later he visited Moscow where he actually managed to persuade Brezhnev in principle to negotiate with the United States on the crucial question of intermediate nuclear missiles, although little was achieved in subsequent talks in Madrid, 1980–83.

It is arguable that *Ostpolitik* by 1980 was beginning to degenerate into an open appeasement of Moscow and the Eastern European regimes. Bonn did not join London and Washington in criticising the Russian invasion of Afghanistan or the Polish government's reaction to *Solidarity*. Indeed no less a person than Willy Brandt actually condemned *Solidarity* for threatening the stability of the Polish regime! When martial law was declared by the Polish government in Poland in December 1981, Schmidt went out of his way to avoid criticising it. He was unwilling to sacrifice what had already been achieved by *Ostpolitik* in improving relations between the two Germanies for the sake of the Poles. By the time the Pershing and Cruise missiles were deployed in the FRG in November 1983 Schmidt had been replaced by Kohl, who also took great care to minimise the impact of this action on *Ostpolitik*.

5 Gorbachev and the End of the Cold War in Europe, 1985–91

> **KEY ISSUES** Why did Gorbachev want to end the Cold War and did he end it in the way he intended?

After Brezhnev's death in 1983, there were already signs that the Soviet leadership wished to resume its policy of *détente* with the USA and start the difficult of task of making the Soviet economy more competitive with the West (see page 116). His two immediate successors, Yuri Andropov and Konstantin Chernenko, were old, sick men, and it was not until Mikhail Gorbachev came to power in 1985 that real changes could be effectively implemented. Gorbachev inherited a difficult situation:

- The collapse of *détente* in the late 1970s between the US and USSR had led to a new and expensive arms race. In 1983 President Reagan announced the development of 'Star Wars' or SDI, the Strategic Defence Initiative, which was a plan for setting up nuclear and laser-armed satellites. These would be able to destroy ballistic missiles in the atmosphere and therefore make the USA safe from a Soviet attack. Moscow lacked both the financial means as well as the technology to build a rival system and feared that SDI might tempt the USA to launch a pre-emptive nuclear strike on the USSR.
- The USSR, like the USA in the 1960s, was increasingly suffering from 'global over-stretch'. It was fighting an unwinnable war in Afghanistan and was giving financial and military aid to left-wing regimes in Angola and the Horn of Africa. All of this cost a great deal of money.
- The Soviet economy was stagnating and desperately needed both technological and financial input from the West. Since 1975 its industrial production rate had been dropping and it was far behind the West in developing the new technologies.

It was clearly therefore in the USSR's interests to restore the Soviet-Western *détente* and resume negotiations on the reduction of armaments, but Gorbachev wished to go further than that. He was determined to end the Cold War because waging it was too costly and stopped him from implementing his policies of *Perestroika* and *Glasnost*, that is fundamentally reforming the Soviet economy and liberalising the Soviet political system. Unlike Stalin, Khrushchev and Brezhnev, he did not conduct Soviet foreign policy according to the Marxist–Leninist revolutionary ideology (see page 3). He no longer believed that Communism would eventually triumph over the West. Instead he worked towards achieving international cooperation and a real coexistence between the two hitherto rival systems, whose values and principles would in time converge rather than conflict. In 1994 an American historian, R.L. Garthoff, described the new Gorbachev doctrine as representing

a shift of policy and performance, disengaging by choice from a whole global confrontation with the United States, to a policy predicated [based] on cooperative security and normalised relations with other countries'.[10]

a) *Détente* Renegotiated, 1985–8

Although the decision had been taken to renew arms talks only months before Gorbachev came to power, he quickly showed that he was determined to negotiate major reductions in nuclear weapons. In April 1985 he stopped increasing the number of SS-20s being installed in Eastern Europe, and in October actually started to reduce the total number deployed. He failed at the Reykjavik Conference in 1986 to persuade Reagan to give up the SDI plan in return for the negotiation of arms control treaties. However, such was his wish to end the arms race that he accepted unconditionally the NATO plan for a total withdrawal of medium range missiles by both sides in Europe at the Washington summit in December 1987.

For the next two years Gorbachev showed a determination not just to restore *détente* but to end the Cold War. In February 1988 Soviet troops began to pull out of Afghanistan, and at the United Nations in December he publicly conceded that Marxism-Leninism was not the key to ultimate truth. According to one American Senator this was 'the most astounding statement of surrender in the history of ideological struggle'.[11]

b) Gorbachev and Eastern Europe

By withdrawing from Afghanistan and Africa Gorbachev re-focused Soviet policy on Europe. Again here he hoped to safeguard Soviet security through a policy of political cooperation and negotiation. On 6 July he told the Council of Europe in a famous speech that

> the common European home ... excludes all possibility of armed confrontation, all possibility of resorting to threat or use of force, and notably military force employed by one alliance against another, within an alliance, or whatever it might be.

It is hard to imagine, as Craig Nation has stressed, 'a more straightforward repudiation of the Brezhnev Doctrine' (see pages 116–7).[12]

Gorbachev encouraged the former satellite states to reform and to liberalise. In the USSR in March 1989 there were for the first time multi-candidate elections which led to reformers and dissidents sitting in the Congress of People's Deputies. In Poland *Solidarity* was legalised, elections took place in June and a non-Communist prime minister took power in August, while in Hungary the Communists agreed to multi-party elections – the very demand that had led to Soviet intervention in 1956! It is not surprising that American observers were beginning to come to the conclusion that 'we are quite literally in the early phases of what might be called the post Communist era'.[13]

At first the other satellite states – Bulgaria, Czechoslovakia, the GDR and Romania – attempted to insulate themselves from the consequences of Gorbachev's policies, but in September the GDR was confronted with a major crisis that led not only to the downfall of Communism in Eastern Europe but to the unification of Germany and the end of the Cold War.

c) The Collapse of the GDR

The GDR was a product of the Cold War, and to survive into the Gorbachev era it needed to win the loyalty of its population, as it could no longer appeal to Soviet power to maintain law and order. By the summer of 1989 it seemed unlikely that it would be able to achieve this. Its economy, like the USSR's, suffered from centralised planning and a top heavy system of bureaucratic control. Ironically only massive West German loans in 1983–4 had saved it from bankruptcy.

The GDR faced a major challenge when the Hungarian Government decided in August to open its frontiers with Austria and some 150,000 East Germans poured across the border on their

By February 1990 GDR troops had already started to demolish the Berlin Wall.

way to the FRG. Under pressure from Kohl, Honecker also granted exit visas to the thousands of East Germans who had travelled to Poland and Prague, and who were quite literally besieging the West German embassies there in a desperate attempt to flee the GDR. Honecker was now facing a crisis potentially every bit as grave as Ulbricht had in 1961 (see page 104). His belated grants of exit visas did nothing to restore confidence in the GDR. On the contrary it merely made his handling of the crisis look unsure. In Leipzig a series of large but peaceful demonstrations took place in late September and early October, which the regime reluctantly tolerated because it knew that Gorbachev would not support a hard-line policy. Indeed when Gorbachev visited Berlin on 5 October to attend the celebrations marking the fortieth anniversary, he advised Honecker to follow the example of the Poles and Hungarians and pointedly warned him that 'life punishes latecomers'.[14] In an effort to stabilise the situation Honecker was sacked, and on 8 November the Berlin Wall was opened. More than anything else this highly symbolic event marked the end of the Cold War. Under the leadership of Hans Modorow the GDR then rapidly followed the example of Poland and agreed to free elections, which were held in March 1990. The 'Alliance for Germany' coalition, which supported reunification won a majority of seats, and on 12 April the new Government announced that it wished to join the FRG.

d) The Other Eastern European States

In Bulgaria and Czechoslovakia events followed very much the same pattern as in the GDR. Peaceful demonstrations forced the replacement of the Communist government by new multi-party regimes. As the old Soviet Bloc disintegrated, Gorbachev resolutely refused to intervene. His spokesman Gennadii Gerasimov startled the West when he said that the Brezhnev doctrine had been replaced the 'Frank Sinatra doctrine'. By this he was referring to the singer's signature ballad, 'I did it my way',[15] implying that the Eastern European states should be allowed to determine their own future. Only in Romania was there any attempt to resist the tide of *glasnost* sweeping over Eastern Europe. Here Nicolae Ceausescu, the Communist dictator, made several attempts to break up demonstrations, which led to escalating violence. In December after a violent clash between the army, which had come out against the regime, and the security forces, he was arrested and executed together with his wife.

Given these dramatic events in the second half of 1989, it is not surprising that the American President George Bush and Gorbachev agreed, when they met at Malta in December, that the Cold War was over.

6 Unification of Germany

> **KEY ISSUE** How was Germany reunified?

The end of the Cold War still left the future of Germany undecided. At first neither the USSR nor Britain nor France wanted a united Germany, and Chancellor Kohl himself was thinking only of forming a very loose confederation which would very slowly grow into a political union, but the strength of East German public opinion in the winter of 1989–90 convinced him that unity was the only option. The division of Germany had marked the beginning of the Cold War. Its reunification marked the real end of the Cold War.

Kohl could not re-unify Germany without the agreement of the USSR, America and Germany's main Western European allies, Britain and France. However, only the USSR and America had the power to stop it. Thus the real negotiations were between Bonn, Moscow and Washington. At first Gorbachev was opposed to the liquidation of the GDR, and in December 1989 promised that he would 'see to it that no harm comes to the GDR'.[16] Yet by the end of January his support for it was ebbing rapidly. On 10 February he told Kohl in Moscow that the Germans themselves should decide on the question of German unity, and at Ottowa four days later President Bush also gave the green light and outlined a formula for proceeding with the negotiations, the Two-Plus-Four talks, which would bring together both the two Germanies and the four former occupying powers which still had residual rights in Berlin. In a series of negotiations in Bonn, Berlin, Paris and Moscow in the summer of 1990 German unity was brokered. Any lingering Russian opposition to German unity and the membership of a united Germany in NATO was overcome by generous West German loans, which Gorbachev hoped would facilitate the modernisation of the Russian economy. Opposition in the West, particularly in London and Paris, was stilled by Kohl's insistence on Germany's continued membership of NATO and on the incorporation of East Germany into the EC (the European Community).

On 12 September the Two-Plus-Four Treaty was signed in Moscow. It was in effect a peace treaty ending the partition of Germany, as it terminated the remaining rights of the former occupying powers in Germany and committed the new Germany to recognisng the Oder-Neisse border with Poland. At midnight on 2 October 1990 the GDR was integrated into the FRG and a re-united Germany came into existence. The West had indeed won a spectacular victory.

7 Assessment

> **KEY ISSUES** Why was Cold War Europe so stable for so long and why did this stability break down by 1989?

Writing in 1987 John Gaddis argued the Cold War had brought a 'long peace' to Europe.[17] Certainly from 1963 onwards Europe was a stable and peaceful, although divided, continent. Even the 'New Cold War' of the early 1980s did not really see a return to the tensions of the Stalinist and Khrushchev eras. Stability during this period rested on two main foundations:

- mutually agreed nuclear arms control between the two Superpowers at a level where each could deter the other from risking war,

- and in Europe the *Ostpolitik* pursued by the FRG since 1969, which for the foreseeable future appeared to have regulated the German question.

What brought this 'long peace' to a close was essentially the collapse of the centralised Soviet command economy, which had squandered enormous sums on nuclear armaments and failed to restructure itself to face the economic challenges of the 1970s and 1980s. The USSR, weakened by the renewed arms race, the flare up of ethnic conflicts within its borders and virtually bankrupt, was no longer in the position to enforce the Brezhnev doctrine. Gorbachev thus had little option but to wind up the Cold War, seek Western credits and try to modernise the Soviet economy by the partial introduction of free market principles. He hoped that a reformed and economically strengthened USSR would be able to forge new links of genuine friendship with the Eastern European states. He did not foresee that by December 1991 real political power in Moscow would lie with an elected president and that the USSR would be replaced by the establishment of a Commonwealth of Independent states. His resignation on 25 December marked the end of the USSR.

References

1 A.J. Nicholls, *The Bonn Republic* (Longman, 1997), p. 232.
2 T. Garton Ash, *In Europe's Name* (Vintage, 1994), p. 71.
3 L. Bark and D.R. Gress, *History of West Germany, Vol. 2* (Blackwell, 1993), p. 194.
4 Garton Ash, *op.cit.*, p. 78.
5 R.L. Hutchings, *Soviet–East European Relations* (Madison, Wisconsin, 1983), p. 94.
6 M. Walker, *The Cold War* (Vintage, 1994), p. 229.
7 *Ibid.*, p. 237.
8 *Ibid.*, p. 218.
9 Garton Ash, *op.cit.*, p. 166.
10 R.L. Garthoff, *The Great Transition: American–Soviet Relations and the End of the Cold War* (The Brookings Institution, 1994), p. 748, quoted in G. Roberts, *The Soviet Union in World Politics* (Routledge, 1999), p. 95.
11 T. Blanton, 'When Did the Cold War End?' *Cold War International History Project Bulletin (CWIHP)* (Woodrow Wilson International Centre for Scholars, Washington, DC.) at cwihp.si.edu, p. 1.

12 R. Craig Nation, *Black Earth, Red Star* (Cornell UP, 1992), p. 308, quoted in Blanton, *op.cit.*, p. 2.
13 A comment by Z. Brzezinski in Blanton, *op.cit.*, p. 2.
14 Quoted in Roberts, *op.cit.*, p. 97.
15 Blanton, *op.cit.*, p. 2.
16 Garton Ash, *op.cit.*, p. 349.
17 J.L. Gaddis, *The Long Peace: Inquiries into the History of the Cold War* (OUP, New York, 1987).

Summary Diagram
The Cold War in Europe, 1963–1991

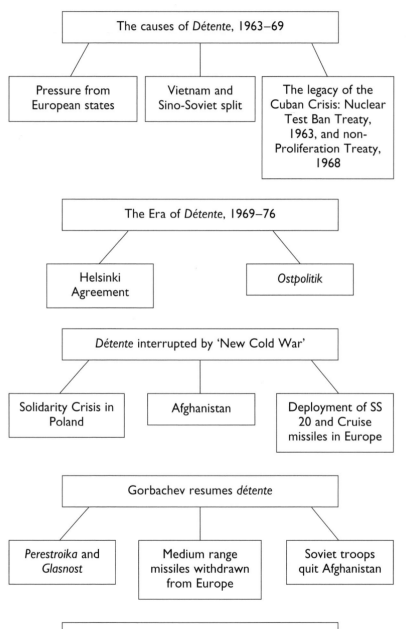

Working on Chapter 7

This chapter covers a long period. In noting it you first of all need to make sure that you know what the word *détente* means. Then write down a list of the reasons why both the Western Powers and the USSR pursued *détente*. In Europe the most important achievement of this policy was the treaties negotiated by Willy Brandt in 1970–73 as part of his *Ostpolitik* and then the Helsinki final Act of 1975. You will need to note all these agreements carefully together with the Four Power Treaty on Berlin and show why they can be regarded as a turning point in the history of the Cold War. Again ask yourself who benefited most from this cluster of treaties. Was the Helsinki Agreement a 'second Yalta' (see pages 28–9), or did it help subtly undermine the Soviet Bloc? In the last sections of the chapter there are three questions to answer: Why did the 'New Cold War' break out? Was it really a 'new' Cold War and why within a few years of its end had the Soviet bloc and the USSR disintegrated?

Answering structured and essay questions on Chapter 7

1. **a)** Outline briefly Willy Brandt's *Ostpolitik* over the period 1969–73.
   b) In what ways can this be seen as a turning point in the German question?
   c) What did the USSR hope to gain from Brandt's *Ostpolitik*?
2. **a)** Outline briefly the main points of the Helsinki Agreement.
   b) Why has it been called the 'centrepiece of Soviet and East European diplomacy in the 1970s'?
   c) Would you agree with those Western politicians who called it a 'second Yalta'?

The first two sets of structured questions require precise and relatively brief answers. The questions range from the purely factual as in 1a) and 2a) to ones which demand a more analytical and thoughtful response. For instance when you are answering 1c) it is no good just writing out a narrative account of the Treaties of 1970–73. You must, instead, think carefully what the USSR wanted to achieve through these negotiations, and show how and why it hoped that the treaties would consolidate its grip on Eastern Europe.

Here are some further examples of essay questions which are much more open-ended and are concerned with a wider sweep of time and events:

1. '*Détente* does not mean the end of danger ... *détente* is not the same as lasting peace'. Do you agree that the development of the Cold War from 1963 to 1989 shows how accurate this observation by President Nixon was?

2. In what ways can the Cold War in Europe between 1963 and 1989 be called the 'long peace'?

3. Was the 'New Cold War' really 'new'?

Before planning your answers to these, make sure you are aware of the relevant facts and problems of the period covered by the question. Sometimes misleadingly simple sounding questions target complex historical problems as in question 3, for instance. As we have seen, a familiar device used by examiners is to give you a quotation and ask you to comment on it with reference to a particular period of time. Thus here in question 1 you must test the accuracy of Nixon's comment by actually looking at the events of the 1970s and 1980s. This does not, of course, mean that you should just 'tell the story' of this period. You must analyse *the events in light of the question set*, but you do not have to agree with the comment, provided that you can back up your counter-arguments with convincing evidence. Question 2 is a complex question covering a sweep of 26 years. Its defining words are 'long peace'. It would help you to plan your answer if you remembered that John Gaddis used this term in 1987 to explain how the Cold War in Europe had settled down after the Cuban crisis into a relatively stable international system. Do you agree with Gaddis' assessment? Was the situation really stable or was Nixon more perceptive about its dangers? By the time you come to plan Question 3 you will have already thought about the increasing tension in Europe during the period 1978–85. Was this a 'new' Cold War or simply a phase in the old one? To answer this you will need to look at these years in the context of the whole Cold War in Europe. What was the Cold War really about in Europe? Were those issues still alive in the early 1980s? Was the 'New Cold War' perhaps just a flare up of old tensions?

Source-based questions on Chapter 7

1 The Limits to Détente

Carefully read the extracts on pages 115, 116 and 122. Answer the following questions:

a) Study the extract on page 115.
   i) What is meant by 'collective defence' (line 1)? (*2 marks*)
   ii) How does the author of this source think that NATO can contribute to the process of *détente*? (*3 marks*)

b) Study the extract on page 116.
   i) What is meant by 'hostile forces pushing your country off the road of Socialism' (lines 1–2)? (*3 marks*)
   ii) To what extent does this source explain why Warsaw Pact forces invaded Czechoslovakia in the night of 20–21 August 1968? Explain your answer fully. (*5 marks*)

c) Study the extract on page 122.
  i) Explain what is meant by 'counterrevolutionary forces' (line 2). (*2 marks*)
  ii) Assess the value of this source to historians studying the international impact of the crisis in Poland 1980–81. (*5 marks*)
d) Study all three extracts and use your own knowledge.
  i) Does a study of these sources and your own knowledge suggest that *détente* was simply a recognition by the Western Powers of Soviet influence in Eastern Europe and not a real peace at all? Explain your answer fully. (*10 marks*)

2 The End of the Cold War
Read carefully the extracts on pages 124 and 125 and study the illustration on page 126.

a) Study the extract on page 124.
  i) What does the author mean by 'global confrontation' (line 2)? (*3 marks*)
  ii) What does the author mean by 'cooperative security and normalised relations with other countries' (line 3)? (*3 marks*)
b) Study the extract on page 125.
  i) What does Gorbachev mean by 'the common European home' (line 1)? (*3 marks*)
  ii) Does this extract indicate that Gorbachev is signalling the end of the Cold War? Explain your answer fully. (*5 marks*)
c) Study the illustration on page 126.
  i) Assess the value of this source to historians studying the history of the Cold War. (*6 marks*)
d) Using these documents and your own knowledge to explain how Gorbachev's foreign policy differed from Brezhnev's. (*10 marks*)

8 Conclusion: The Cold War, 1945–91

POINTS TO CONSIDER

This chapter is a general survey of the Cold War concentrating on the main issues which anybody studying the period needs to think about. Your aim should be to consolidate your overall knowledge and understanding of the whole period with particular focus on key problems and trends.

The Cold War in Europe lasted for over four decades and by the mid 1960s the divisions that had grown out of the immediate postwar years were accepted as a permanent fact of international life. Twenty years later, as we have seen, the American historian, John Gaddis, was able to describe the uneasy stability that it had created as 'the long peace'. It was, however, more a truce than a peace. Even at the height of *détente* during the 1970s tension, hostility and competition still characterised the relations between the Warsaw Pact and NATO states.

1 Could the Cold War Have Been Avoided?

KEY ISSUE What caused the Cold War?

Revisionist historians like Daniel Yergin and Willy Loth[1] argue that it was the USA that provoked the Cold War by refusing to recognise the Soviet sphere of interest in Eastern Europe or to make concessions over reparations in Germany. Could the Cold War really have been avoided if Stalin had been treated more diplomatically and greater sympathy shown to the appalling postwar problems in the USSR? It is possible to make out a case that Stalin did in fact act with greater restraint in Eastern Europe than his later Cold War critics in the West gave him credit for. He stopped Tito from intervening in Greece and, until 1948, allowed semi-democratic regimes to function in Hungary and Czechoslovakia. Loth argues that initially he also tried to restrain his own military government officials in the Soviet Zone of Germany from applying too rigidly the Soviet Communist model. Indeed it is arguable that up to the Summer of 1947 Stalin gave precedence to trying to maintain the wartime Grand Alliance and failed to exploit favourable opportunities for establishing Soviet influence in such areas as Iran and Greece.

Was it then British and American policy that caused the Cold War? Can Stalin really be regarded as an innocent party pushed into waging the Cold War by the manoeuverings of the Anglo-Americans? Revisionist historians point to the determination of the Americans to deny the Soviets access to raw materials in the Western hemisphere and of British attempts to force a decision on the future of Germany, which would almost inevitably lead to its division. There is no doubt that initially Stalin's policy was 'moderate' in that he did not want a third world war, as the USSR was hardly in the position to wage it. Yet what in retrospect can be called moderation did not necessarily seem to be so at the time. The British and Americans were alarmed by Soviet requests for control of the Black Sea Straits and of the former Italian colony of Libya. Even though Stalin withdrew these, they were seen as evidence of expansionist tendencies. Similarly the exclusion of Western influence from Poland and most of Eastern Europe seemed to be an aggressive act and fed suspicions in London and Washington of Soviet actions. There was an ambiguity about Soviet policy. Stalin's ruthless suppression of all opposition in Poland and the 'shot-gun marriage' of the SPD and SED in the Soviet Zone in Germany in 1946 alienated politicians in London and Washington even when he still hoped to work closely with them. On the other hand London and Washington also gave out conflicting signals. They resented being excluded from Eastern Europe, but in their turn excluded the USSR from Western Europe and the Mediterranean.

Great power rivalry, mutual fears about security and rival ideologies were all causes of the Cold War. Stalin's personality, too, is relevant, and it is arguable that the Cold War was an extension of the same distrust and suspicion which characterised his domestic policy. According to Gaddis, 'he functioned in much the same manner whether operating within the international system, within his alliances, within his country ... or party. [He] waged war on all these fronts. The Cold War we came to know was only one of many from his point of view'.[2]

2 When Did the Cold War Actually Start?

> **KEY ISSUE** Why is there a debate about when the Cold War started?

As we have seen in Chapter One, historians disagree about when to date the beginning of the Cold War. Relations between the Western Powers, particularly the USA and the USSR, had been deteriorating ever since the defeat of Hitler, which had been the main cement holding together the Grand Alliance. The Cold War has been dated variously from the dropping of the atom bombs on Hiroshima and Nagasaki, Churchill's famous Iron Curtain speech in March 1946 or the launching of the Truman doctrine in March 1947. Although the beginnings of the Cold War are hard to pinpoint, it was certainly well under way by the end of 1947. The withdrawal of the USSR from the

Paris talks on Marshall Aid, the creation of the Cominform and the breakdown of the London Conference were important stages in the escalation of the Cold War in that year.

3 The Cold War in Europe

> **KEY ISSUE** Why was Europe the main theatre of the Cold War?

Europe was the main, although not the only, theatre of the Cold War. It was there that it both began and ended. For the USSR it was essential to keep Eastern Europe under its control as a protective barrier against any possible attack from the West. It was this fact that led to Soviet intervention in Hungary in 1956 and to the formulation of the Brezhnev doctrine 12 years later. The prize that both sides struggled for was Germany. In this the Western powers had the advantage as they controlled two-thirds of the country, which included the great industrial centre of the Ruhr. The military and economic integration of the Western two thirds of Germany into Western Europe was what Stalin most dreaded. The Berlin blockade was an attempt to stop this from happening, but it merely intensified Western efforts to create an independent West German state in 1949. Again, to prevent West Germany from joining NATO and/or the EDC, Stalin orchestrated a massive peace movement, and finally, as a last desperate try, he actually proposed in March 1952 a plan for creating a neutral and apparently free Germany. In 1953 Beria very briefly played with the possibility of 'selling' the GDR to West Germany subject to certain restrictions on its armaments, but after the East German uprising of 1953, this idea was quickly dropped and until 1989 Soviet policy was to build up the weak and vulnerable East German state.

The division of Germany mirrored the division of Europe. The construction of the Berlin Wall confirmed the division of Germany for another 28 years, and in time brought a certain stability to Central Europe. The only problem was that in the long term the division was unstable or asymmetrical. As President Eisenhower's National Security Council pointed out, the FRG had 'had nearly three times the population, about five times the industrial output and almost twice the size'[3] of the GDR. Similarly Western Europe and the USA together represented infinitely more economic power than the Soviet bloc could command.

The same lack of symmetry can be seen in the way the two Superpowers influenced their respective blocs. On balance it is true to say that the USA initially set up in Western Europe an 'empire by invitation'.[4] The Western Europeans in the late 1940s were desperate for American military and financial aid. On the other hand in Eastern Europe, with the partial exceptions of Hungary and

Czechoslovakia until 1947, the USSR established an empire by conquest.

In the Soviet Zone of Germany the behaviour of the Red Army and the mass raping carried out by its soldiers in 1945 created an atmosphere of hate and fear, which reinforced West Germany's determination to remain within the American sphere of influence at all costs. Essentially the Americans helped create an independent prosperous, economically and increasingly politically integrated Western Europe functioning within a capitalist global system. The Soviets had little to offer Eastern Europe that could rival this. Hence the economic strength of Western Europe exerted a magnetic attraction on the peoples of Eastern Europe.

4 Why Did the Cold War in Europe Last so Long?

> **KEY ISSUE** Could the Cold War have ended before 1989?

If the West had such a significant advantage over the Soviet Bloc, why did the Cold War last so long? It is possible to argue that its eventual outcome should have been predicted as early as 1968 when the crushing of the Prague Spring forced the Czech government and the other satellite states to abandon their attempts to liberalise their economies and to return instead to a system of more rigid centralised control, which made them less flexible and responsive to change. Yet it still seemed inconceivable that the USSR and its Eastern European satellites would eventually collapse like a row of dominoes. The USSR seemed to be a Superpower at least as strong as the USA. This overestimation of its power was caused by assessing its strength solely in terms of its nuclear weapons. This was the one area where it could effectively compete with the West. The long period of *détente* preserved the Soviet nuclear deterrent, but only slowed down its economic decline, despite massive loans from the West.

5 Why Did the Cold War End?

> **KEY ISSUE** What factors caused the end of the Cold War in 1989?

Behind the nuclear facade the whole Soviet bloc was suffering a steady economic, ideological, moral and cultural decline. This was primarily caused by its own economic inefficiencies and inability to match the West's economic growth. *Détente*, the Helsinki agreement and *Ostpolitik* increasingly exposed the Soviet empire to Western influences. As Gaddis has put it:

1 To visualize what happened, imagine a troubled triceratops [a plant eating dinosaur]. From the outside, as rivals contemplated its sheer size, tough skin, bristling armament and aggressive posturing, the beast looked sufficiently formidable that none dared tangle with it.
5 Appearances deceived, though, for within, its digestive, circulatory and respiratory systems were slowly clogging up, and then shutting down. There were few external signs of this until the day the creature was found with all four feet in the air still awesome but now bloated stiff, and quite dead. The moral of the fable is that armaments make impress-
10 ive exoskeletons [a rigid external covering for the body], but a shell alone ensures the survival of no animal and no state.

Until the Reagan Presidency no statesman in the West dared call the USSR's bluff. After all, even if the USA had a greater nuclear arsenal, the USSR had the capacity to land, at the very least, a few missiles on America, and that was still a formidable deterrent. By developing the SDI Reagan challenged the USSR in a way that had not happened since the late 1940s. The USSR simply could not keep pace. This was the context in which Gorbachev came to the conclusion that the only chance the USSR had of surviving was to modernise its economy and society along Western lines. He thus embarked on an ambitious but ultimately unsuccessful attempt to base the USSR's links with its satel-lite states on consent rather than coercion. This approach, however, came too late. In 1968 many East Europeans could perhaps still have been won over by the prospect of 'Socialism with a human face', but 20 years later all socialist idealism had evaporated. After the grey, cor-rupt and repressive years of the Brezhnev era, the sudden freedom offered by Gorbachev was used by the Eastern Europeans to reject Socialism and look to the American and Western European economic models.

References

1   D. Yergin, *The Shattered Peace* (Houghton Miflin, 1977) and W. Loth, *Stalin's Unwanted Child: The Soviet Union, the German Question and the Founding of the GDR* (Macmillan, 1998).
2   J.L. Gaddis, *We Now Know: Rethinking Cold War History* (OUP, 1997), p. 293.
3   *Ibid.*, p. 136.
4   This refers to the article 'Empire by Invitation' by G. Lundestad, *Journal of Peace Research*, vol. 23 (Sept. 1986), pp. 263–77.

Summary diagram
Historical Debates about the Cold War in Europe

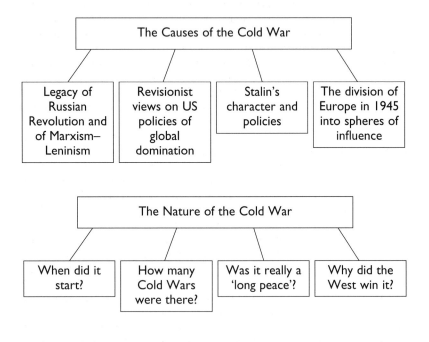

Answering essay questions on Chapter 8

The following are examples of essay questions covering the whole of the Cold War in Europe:

1. Why did the Cold War in Europe last so long?
2. Why did the USA and its Western allies win the Cold War in Europe?
3. To what extent was the Cold War in Europe a 'bipolar struggle' dominated by the USSR and USA?
4. Why was the German question such an important issue in The Cold War?

Ideally you should never be surprised by an essay question in an exam. When you revise, always try to understand what the underlying issues of a particular topic are, before beginning to master the mass of factual detail. If you have done that with the Cold War, the above questions should not surprise you. Once you have thought through one leading question very carefully, you will find that the next question will not be so difficult as there will be some factual and thematic overlap.

Obviously the first essay title is a leading question about the Cold War. The key words here are 'so long'. To answer it you need briefly to discuss how the Soviet and Western blocs reflected the balance of forces in 1945 and how the USSR was determined never again to allow an attack to be launched on it through Eastern Europe. It was therefore in the strategic interests of the USSR to dominate the Eastern European states as long as it could. This can be seen in Khrushchev's reaction to the Hungarian revolt in 1956 and the formulation of the Brezhnev doctrine in 1968. The USSR had sufficient force to do this. Its land forces vastly outnumbered the Western armies, and after 1949, when it exploded its first nuclear bomb, war against the USSR was too great a risk for the West to undertake. Hence there was little real alternative to an armed truce. Yet we have seen that increasingly the USSR was like a triceratops with a tough skin but decaying internal organs. Why then did the Cold War not end in the middle 1950s or 1960s? The answer is that the Western Alliance believed that the USSR would rather go to war than see its vital interests in Eastern Europe suffer. The long period of *détente* was particularly advantageous to the USSR, as it preserved its status as a great power, while Willy Brandt's *Ostpolitik* brought recognition of the GDR and the postwar frontiers of Poland and Czechoslovakia. Finally you must not forget that the Cold war was also an ideological struggle. Both sides were determined to defend their core beliefs in the areas of Europe they influenced.

In the next question the key word is 'win'. To answer this you need to explain how the 'West' controlled, or had access to, the most prosperous and dynamic areas of the world. The most wealthy two thirds of Germany was, for example, firmly economically, politically and militarily integrated into Western Europe. The magnetism that this could exert on the East can be seen in the way millions of East Germans fled the GDR to the FRG until the construction of the Wall in 1961. You will also need to explain how, after the collapse of the 'Prague Spring', the states of the Soviet bloc virtually gave up attempts to modernise and liberalise their economies. They returned, instead, to the old fashioned and rigid neo-Stalinist system where all economic decisions were controlled from the centre by the government. By the end of the seventies their economies were facing major crises. The GDR, for example, was by this stage only kept solvent by huge loans from the FRG. The USSR also had to pay for its massive intervention into Afghanistan and then was faced with Reagan's SDI challenge. Gorbachev therefore took a daring but ultimately unsuccessful gamble in his efforts to modernise the USSR and reform its relations with East Europe.

In the third question the key words are 'to what extent' and 'bipolar'. This is a difficult question that spans the whole period of the Cold War. Obviously in the crucial area of nuclear missiles and bombs there was an overwhelming bipolarity, although both France and Britain possessed small nuclear deterrents. The USSR and the USA were, of course, the 'really big brothers', as Chancellor Schmidt said, but right through the whole Cold War there were other players on the stage. In the early period Britain and France played key roles. The former in NATO, the latter in launching European integration through the ECSC and, later, the doomed EDC. In the Sixties the West European states, particularly France, distanced themselves from the USA, which suffered defeat in Vietnam and subsequent serious economic difficulties. The FRG also seized the initiative in launching its highly sucessful *Ostpolitik* in 1970–72. In the Soviet Bloc there was also more diversity than initially appeared. Tito went his own way in 1948 and was a considerable influence on Khrushchev in 1956. Gomulka carved out an element of independence for himself and Ulbricht was able to bring a certain amount of pressure to bear on Khrushchev during the period 1960–1. On the other hand in 1989 Gorbachev alone took the initiative to end the Cold War without any discussions within the Warsaw Pact. The consent of the USA and USSR was also crucial for the re-unification of Germany in 1990.

The fourth question targets the pivotal role of Germany in the Cold War. Here you need to stress the position of Germany in the middle of Europe, its enormous economic potential and large population. Essentially, whichever bloc possessed it was in a powerful position to win the Cold War. That was why Stalin tried to prevent the Western Zones, in which most of Germany's heavy industry was located, from being formed into the FRG in 1948/49 by launching the Berlin blockade. By the same token it was also why Britain and America wanted West Germany included in NATO. To stop this from happening Stalin proposed in March 1952 a neutral but reunified Germany. Even when Khrushchev recognised the GDR in 1955, the German question remained one of the flash points of the Cold War. West Berlin was an Allied outpost in the middle of the GDR, in which hundreds of thousands of East Germans could find refuge and be flown to the West. By 1961 this labour drain threatened to destabilise the GDR and bring about its collapse. Hence Khrushchev had little option but to sanction the construction of the Berlin Wall to preserve the existence of the GDR. After 1961 the German question was less acute, but it nevertheless remained of great importance. Willy Brandt attempted to normalise relations between the two Germanies with his *Ostpolitik*, but the future of Germany still remained open, as the FRG did not ultimately give up its aim of uniting the two states. Then with the collapse of Communism in 1989–90, the reunification of Germany was one of the most urgent questions facing the USSR and the Western states.

Glossary

ACC   Allied Control Commissions. These were set up in the liberated territories, 1943–5, and in effect governed them.

Axis Powers   Nazi Germany's allies.

Benelux   The states of Belgium, Holland and Luxemburg.

Bizonia   In January 1947 the British and American zones in Germany were amalgamated economically and called Bizonia or the Bizone.

Bloc   A combination of states linked militarily, politically and economically. Hence Eastern and Western blocs in Europe.

Bourgeois Parties Middle class political parties.

CIA   Central Intelligence Agency. The American espionage and security organisation.

Collectivisation The replacement of private farms by agricultural cooperatives.

COMECON   The Council For Mutual Economic Assistance. This was set up by Stalin in 1949 in response to the European Recovery Programme (Marshall Aid).

COMINFORM   Communist Information Bureau. Set up in 1947 as a successor to the Comintern (Communist International), which had been dissolved in 1943.

Détente   A state of lessened tension or growing relaxation between two states.

Deutschmark   The West German currency introduced in 1948.

ECSC   European Coal and Steel Community created in 1951.

EDC   European Defence Community. Proposed by French Government in 1950. Rejected by French Assembly, August 1954.

E[E]C   European Economic Community (later European Community). Created by the Treaty of Rome in March 1957.

EFTA   European Free Trade Association. Set up in 1959.

FRG   Federal Republic of Germany set up in August 1949.

GDR   German Democratic Republic set up in October 1949.

Grand Alliance The coalition of Great Britain, the USSR and USA in the Second World War.

ICBM   Inter-continental ballistic missile. First launched by USSR in Kazakhstan in August 1957.

Ideology	A system of ideas forming a political, philosphical or economic theory.
IRBM	Intermediate-range ballistic missiles.
Iron Curtain	The phrase used by Churchill in 1946 to describe the frontier between the Soviet and Western blocs in Europe.
Marxism–Leninism	The political philosophy of the USSR deriving from Karl Marx and Lenin.
NATO	North Atlantic Treaty Organisation set up in 1949.
OEEC	Organisation For European Economic Cooperation. The organisation was created in April 1948 to supervise the distribution and use of Marshall Aid.
Ostpolitik	The 'eastern policy' conducted by the FRG towards the GDR and the Eastern Bloc after 1969.
Pleven Plan	The Plan for a European army proposed by the French Prime Minister, René Pleven (see EDC).
Politbureau	The key decision-making body in the USSR and the other Communist states.
Polish October	The restoration of Gomulka to the leadership of the Polish Communist Party and the mobilisation of Polish workers to stop Soviet armed intervention in October 1956.
Prague Spring	The name given to the reforms introduced by Dubcek in Czechoslovakia in 1968.
SALT	Strategic Arms Limitation Treaty.
Satellite State	A state which is dependent on and dominated by a Great Power; for instance, the Eastern European states, 1945–89.
SDI	Strategic Defence Initiative.
Secretary of State	The chief American official in charge of foreign policy.
SED	The Socialist Unity Party of Germany. Created in the Soviet Zone in 1946 through amalgamation of the Socialist and Communist parties.
SPD	Social Democratic Party of Germany.
Supranational	Usually applied to an organisation like the ECSC that has the power to make policy on behalf of the national states which are its members.
USSR	The Union of Soviet Socialist Republics. This was the Communist name for Russia.

Further Reading

There are a growing number of specialised books and articles dealing with all aspects of the Cold War in Europe, as archive material in the USSR and the former satellite states becomes available to historians. Before you read these it is important that you should familiarise yourself first with the general accounts of the period.

Textbooks Covering the Whole Period

All the books recommended below are worth reading, but for different reasons:

J. Laver, C. Rowe and **D. Williamson**, *Years of Division Since 1945* (Hodder & Stoughton, 1999) has some very useful introductory chapters on the Cold War, Germany, the USSR and Eastern Europe.

J.W. Mason, *The Cold War, 1945–91* (Routledge, 1996) is an excellent introductory survey of just 75 pages.

G. Roberts, *The Soviet Union in World Politics: Coexistence, Revolution and Cold War, 1945–91* (Routledge, 1999) is a brief but comprehensive survey of Soviet foreign policy during this period.

M. Walker, *The Cold War* (Vintage, 1994) is a readable, journalistic study of the whole Cold War. It covers all aspects of this struggle and contains much useful information.

J.W. Young, *Cold War Europe, 1945–91* (Arnold, 1996, 2nd edn) has an informative chapter on the Cold War and *détente* and then further useful chapters on European integration, Eastern Europe, the USSR and the main Western European states.

Historiography and Problems of the Cold War

D. Reynolds, ed., *The Origins of the Cold War in Europe: International Perspectives* (Yale UP, 1994) is an excellent survey of the historiography and the international historical debates on the Cold War covering the period 1945–55.

J.L. Gaddis, *We Know Now: Rethinking Cold War History* (OUP, 1997) is an important and readable book, which puts the European Cold War into its global context. It is based as far as possible on recent research.

The Cold War International History Project Bulletin (CWIHP, Woodrow Wilson International Center for Scholars, Washington, DC) has published hundreds of articles and documents from Eastern European and Soviet archives. Its aim is 'to disseminate new information and perspectives on Cold War history emerging from previously inaccessible archives'. What makes it a particularly usable source for 'A' Level students is that it can be accessed on the internet at cwihp.si.edu.

Specialist Studies

The specialised literature on the Cold War is often complex and written primarily for historians and political scientists. However, the following are some suggested starting points for further study, which are not too difficult to read and understand:

a) The Origins of the Cold War up to 1953

M. McCauley, *The Origins of the Cold War, 1941–49* (Longman, 1995, 2nd edn) is a clear and well explained introduction to the causes and early stages of the Cold War.

M. Leffler and **D.S. Painter**, *Origins of the Cold War* (Routledge, 1994) contains a number of interesting essays on different aspects of the early Cold War, which represent various conflicting interpretations.

C.M. Maier ed., *The Cold War in Europe* (Markus Wiener 3rd edn, 1996) again has a collection of essays representing contradictory views on the Cold War.

D. Yergin, *Shattered Peace; The Origins of the Cold War and the National Security State* (Houghton Mifflin Company, 1977) is a revisionist study of America's involvement in the Cold War in Europe.

b) The Khrushchev Years, 1953–64

M. McCauley, *The Khrushchev Era* (Longman, 1995) is a clear, concise study of this dramatic period.

c) *Détente* and *Ostpolitik*

M. Bowker and **P. Williams**, *Superpower Détente: A Reappraisal* (Sage, 1988) gives a full account of *détente* in the 1970s.

T. Garton Ash, *In Europe's Name: Germany and the Divided Continent* (Jonathan Cape, 1993) is a very useful guide to *Ostpolitik* and the reunification of Germany.

d) East Europe

J. Laver, *The Eastern and Central European States, 1945–92* (Hodder & Stoughton, 1999) provides a clear guide to the East European states.

G. Swain and **N. Swain**, *Eastern Europe since 1945* (Macmillan, 1993) is a fuller study of the same subject.

e) The End of the Cold War

T. Garton Ash, *We the People – The Revolution of 1990* (Penguin, 1990) is a journalist's account of the collapse of Communism in East Europe.

R. Garthoff, *The Great Transition: American-Soviet Relations and the End of the Cold War* (Brookings Institution, Washington, 1994) is a difficult but important book on the end of the Cold War.

Index

and riots (June 1953) 82–4,
91
and the Berlin Crisis
(1958–61) 99–104, 106
and *Ostpolitik* 119–20, 123
and Poland 100, 122
collapse of 126–28
Germany
defeat and occupation of
28–30, 38–41
reparations from 36, 40–2,
50, 135
Allied disagreements on 36,
40–2, 60–6
Soviet Zone in 39–40, 56,
65–6
and creation of Bizonia 41
division of 56, 59–60, 65–8
reunification of 65, 74, 79, 85,
87, 128
Germany, Federal Republic of
and rearmament, 73–9, 82,
84–5,
87–8, 90
and *Ostpolitik* 114, 117–21,
123
and Berlin Crisis (1958–61)
102
Gomulka, Wladyslaw 46, 58, 93,
105, 109
Gorbachev, Mikhail 116, 123–29,
139, 141
Greece 5, 19–20, 24–5, 135

Hallstein Doctrine 87, 118
Helsinki Final Act 120–1, 132, 138
Hitler, Adolf 5, 50, 136
Honecker, Erich 119
Hungary 8, 19, 25, 37, 45, 47–8,
58, 125–6
and revolt in 95–7, 109, 115,
137, 146

'Iron Curtain' 45, 53
Italy 20, 27–8, 42, 49

Kennedy, John 103–05

Khrushchev, Nikita
and destalinisation 8, 81,
93–4, 98
and the revolts (1956) 9,
95–7, 109
and 'nuclear diplomacy' 97–8
and the GDR 87, 99–104, 142
and the Berlin Crisis
(1958–61) 99–104
and Cuba 105–07, 113
Korean War 75, 77

Lenin, Vladimir 2, 4

Marshall Plan 43–5, 57, 77, 80,
137
Marx, Karl 2

NATO 8, 64, 76–8, 80, 84–5, 64,
70–1, 73–4, 84, 88, 98,
114–15, 122, 125, 135, 137
Nixon, President Richard
117–18, 132–3
nuclear weapons 10–11, 36–7,
74, 77, 97, 105–06,113,
122–4, 138–9, 141

Ostpolitik 9, 117–18, 123, 129,
132

Poland 8, 20, 21–2, 36, 45–6, 50,
112, 95, 98, 100, 106, 109,
115, 118, 125
and the *Solidarity* movement
122–3, 125

Reagan, President Ronald 2,
123, 125, 139, 141
Romania 19–20, 22–4, 37–8,
46–7, 50, 127
Roosevelt, President Franklin
18–19, 22, 28, 29–30, 34
Ruhr 60, 75, 87, 137

Schuman Plan 74–5, 90
Socialist Unity Party (SED)
39–40, 56, 65–6, 83, 119